Integrated Broadband Networks

An Introduction to ATM-Based Networks

ELECTRONIC SYSTEMS ENGINEERING SERIES

Consulting editors **E L Dagless**
University of Bristol

J O'Reilly
University College of Wales

OTHER TITLES IN THE SERIES

Advanced Microprocessor Architectures   *L Ciminiera and A Valenzano*

Optical Pattern Recognition Using Holographic Techniques   *N Collings*

Modern Logic Design   *D Green*

Data Communications, Computer Networks and OSI (2nd Edn)   *F Halsall*

Multivariable Feedback Design   *J M Maciejowski*

Microwave Components and Systems   *K F Sander*

Tolerance Design of Electronic Circuits   *R Spence and R Soin*

Computer Architecture and Design   *A J van de Goor*

Digital Systems Design with Programmable Logic   *M Bolton*

Introduction to Robotics   *P J McKerrow*

MAP and TOP Communications: Standards and Applications
   A Valenzano, C Demartini and L Ciminiera

Integrated Broadband Networks

An Introduction to ATM-Based Networks

RAINER HÄNDEL
MANFRED N. HUBER

Siemens, Munich

ADDISON-WESLEY
PUBLISHING
COMPANY

Wokingham, England · Reading, Massachusetts · Menlo Park, California · New York
Don Mills, Ontario · Amsterdam · Bonn · Sydney · Singapore
Tokyo · Madrid · San Juan · Milan · Paris · Mexico City · Seoul · Taipei

Cover designed by Chris Eley and
printed by The Riverside Printing Co. (Reading) Ltd.
Printed in Great Britain by The Bath Press, Avon.

First printed 1991. Reprinted 1992 and 1993 (twice).

British Library Cataloguing in Publication Data
Händel, Rainer
    Integrated broadband networks : an introduction
    to ATM-based networks. – (Electronic systems
    engineering series)
    I. Title   II. Huber, Manfred   III. Series
    004.68

    ISBN 0-201-54444-X

Library of Congress Cataloging in Publication Data
Händel, Rainer.
        Integrated broadband networks : an introduction to ATM-based
    networks / Rainer Händel, Manfred N. Huber.
            p.   cm. — (Electronic systems engineering series)
        Includes bibliographical references and index.
        ISBN 0-201-54444-X
        1. Integrated services digital networks. 2. Broadband
    communication systems.   I. Huber, Manfred N.   II. Title.
    III. Series.
    TK5103.7.H364   1991
    621.382—dc20   91-18839
                                                                CIP

Preface

Virtually everyone uses the phone nowadays as a (more or less) efficient communication tool. It provides us with the capability of exchanging information between different places around the world; it is quick due to its real-time operation and it is easy to handle. These assets, namely global availability, short response times and user-friendliness, have made telephony the communication evergreen that is listened to by millions of people around the world every minute.

Engineers developing integrated broadband network concepts and products are dreaming that their ideas will be as successful as plain old telephony was. Of course, not all experts are yet convinced that this will actually happen, nor are potential customers who often do not even know what powerful communication tools the future will offer them.

Integrated broadband networks are being conceived as an extension of 64 kbit/s based integrated services digital networks (ISDNs). These themselves incorporate telephony as one of their main applications; in fact, ISDN is based on the digitized telephone network.

ISDN is an all-digital network; all source information (irrespective of its meaning to the user) is transmitted and switched as digital signals end to end. So a common signal transfer mechanism can be employed in the network to serve several applications that are quite different in nature, e.g. voice and data transmission.

ISDN seems to be a natural development of plain telephony with good prospects to succeed as well.

Broadband integrated services digital networks (B-ISDNs) will add a tremendous new feature to ISDNs: considerably higher bit rates will be available for fast data or moving picture transmission, for example, and these bit rates may be demanded per connection with great flexibility in choosing the value actually needed.

How this will be achieved is described in this book. It introduces the idea of integrated broadband networks, gives a survey of the current situation concerning B-ISDN and provides a detailed technical discussion of broadband networks based on the emerging international standards.

The book will address the following items:

- What broadband capabilities are and where they are needed.

- 'Integrated broadband networks': the original approach to add broadband channels to the 64 kbit/s ISDN and what really happened with B-ISDN.

- The main ingredients of B-ISDN: asynchronous transfer mode (ATM) and optical transmission (synchronous digital hierarchy).

- ATM networking (virtual paths and virtual channels; resource allocation; traffic management; network performance etc.).

- User-network access configurations and interfaces/protocols.

- B-ISDN network equipment: ATM switches, cross-connects and transmission systems.

- How to evolve towards B-ISDN.

- How to integrate existing networks and networks that will probably be implemented before B-ISDN, e.g. metropolitan area networks (MANs).

- B-ISDN trials.

- Possible future development (e.g. Gbit/s systems, optical switching).

Some other ATM-specific problems will also be covered, e.g. voice delay and echo in ATM networks, connectionless service provision and tariffing in ATM networks.

An overview of the current standardization situation is annexed. Reference to the standards documents is made whenever appropriate in the book so that the reader can easily find further information.

The book addresses people involved in the planning, development, implementation and sale of telecommunication networks and terminals. The material presented may also be used for an introductory course into broadband networks in the academic field.

Acknowledgements

The authors appreciate the stimulating and fruitful discussions with all their colleagues. We would also like to express our thanks to A. Biersack, U. Branczik and R. Trox for technical support.

R. Händel
M.N. Huber

June 1991

Contents

Chapter 1

Introduction

1.1   The Current Situation

At present, most networks are dedicated to specific purposes like telephony, TV distribution, circuit-switched or packetized data transfer.

Some applications make use of the widespread telephone network, e.g. facsimile. Using pre-existing networks for new applications may lead to characteristic shortcomings, however, as such networks usually are not tailored to the needs of services that were unknown when the networks were implemented. So data transfer over the telephone network is confined by a lack of bandwidth, flexibility and quality of analog voice transmission equipment. The telephone networks were engineered for a constant bandwidth service, therefore using them for variable bit rate data traffic requires costly adaptation.

Since in general the public telephone network was not able effectively to support non-voice services to an extent that was required by the customer, other dedicated networks arose, e.g. public data networks or private data networks connecting, say, a big company's plants or several research institutes.

Private networks often deploy non-standardized equipment, interfaces and protocols and are unable to offer access to other networks and users. If gateways to the outside world are required, their implementation may be tedious and costly.

Table 1.1 illustrates the variety of existing data transmission schemes. Note that this table contains only standardized user classes according to CCITT Recommendation X.1 [77]. CCITT is the acronym for *Comité Consultatif International Télégraphique et Téléphonique*, which is in charge of setting network standards for public telecommunication.

Class	Bit Rate		Characteristics
1	300	bit/s	Start/Stop mode
2	50 ... 200	bit/s	Start/Stop mode
3	600	bit/s	Synchronous operation mode
4	2400	bit/s	Synchronous operation mode
5	4800	bit/s	Synchronous operation mode
6	9600	bit/s	Synchronous operation mode
7	48000	bit/s	Synchronous operation mode
8	2400	bit/s	CCITT Recommendation X.25 [78]
9	4800	bit/s	CCITT Recommendation X.25
10	9600	bit/s	CCITT Recommendation X.25
11	48000	bit/s	CCITT Recommendation X.25
12	1200	bit/s	CCITT Recommendation X.25
13	64000	bit/s	CCITT Recommendation X.25
19	64000	bit/s	Synchronous operation mode
20	50 ... 300	bit/s	CCITT Recommendation X.28 [79]
21	75 ... 1200	bit/s	CCITT Recommendation X.28
22	1200	bit/s	CCITT Recommendation X.28
23	2400	bit/s	CCITT Recommendation X.28
30	64000	bit/s	ISDN

Table 1.1: *User classes within public data networks*

1.2   The Idea of the Integrated Services Digital Network

In 1984, the Plenary Assembly of the CCITT adopted the I series recommendations dealing with integrated services digital network (ISDN) matters. The CCITT stated that 'an ISDN is a network ... that provides end-to-end digital connectivity to support a wide range of services, including voice and non-voice services, to which users have access by a limited set of standard multi-purpose user-network interfaces' [23]. Such an ISDN standard interface was defined and called *basic access*, comprising two 64 kbit/s B channels and a 16 kbit/s signalling D channel. Another type of interface, the *primary rate access*, with a gross bit rate of about 1.5 Mbit/s or 2 Mbit/s, respectively, offers the flexibility to allocate high speed H channels or mixtures of B and H channels and a 64 kbit/s signalling channel (see Table 1.2).

The ISDN concept laid down in the 1984 recommendations was further elaborated in the meantime; the current status is documented in the 1988 CCITT Blue Books.

This original ISDN is based on the digitized telephone network which is charac-

ISDN Channels		
Channel	Bit Rate	Interface
B	64 kbit/s	Basic access
H0	384 kbit/s	Primary rate access
H11	1536 kbit/s	Primary rate access
H12	1920 kbit/s	Primary rate access
D16	16 kbit/s	Basic access
D64	64 kbit/s	Primary rate access

Interface Structures		
Interface	Gross Bit Rate	Structure
Basic access	192 kbit/s	2B + D16
Primary rate access	1544 kbit/s	23B + D64
		3H0 + D64
		H11
		etc.
Primary rate access	2048 kbit/s	30B + D64
		5H0 + D64
		H12 + D64
		etc.

Table 1.2: *ISDN channels and interface structures*

terized by the 64 kbit/s channel. The channel bit rate of 64 kbit/s is derived from 3.4 kHz voice transmission requirements (8 bit sampling with a frequency of 8 kHz).

The 64 kbit/s ISDN basically is a circuit-switched network but it can offer access to packet-switched services [17].

ISDNs are being implemented in the early 1990s. Their benefits for the user and network provider include [17]:

- A common user-network interface for access to a variety of services

- Enhanced (out-of-band) signalling capabilities

- Service integration

- Provision of new and improved services.

1.3   B-ISDN

The highest bit rate a 64 kbit/s based ISDN can offer to the user is about 1.5 Mbit/s or 2 Mbit/s, respectively, i.e. the H1 channel bit rate (see Table 1.2). Connection of local area networks (LANs), however, or transmission of moving images with good resolution may, in many cases, require considerably higher bit rates (cf. Chapter 2). Consequently, the conception and realization of broadband ISDN (B-ISDN) was desirable.

1.3.1   What is B-ISDN?

CCITT Recommendation I.113 [45] ('Vocabulary of terms for broadband aspects of ISDN') defines *broadband* as:

> *... a service or system requiring transmission channels capable*
> *of supporting rates greater than the primary rate.*

B-ISDN thus includes 64 kbit/s ISDN capabilities but in addition opens the door to applications utilizing bit rates above 1.5 Mbit/s or 2 Mbit/s, respectively. The upper limit of the bit rate available to a broadband user will be somewhat above 100 Mbit/s (see Section 5.2.2).

The above definition of broadband does not indicate how a technical concept of it might or should look like.

Whereas this definition was settled from the beginning, the final technical concept for B-ISDN as described in the following chapters only emerged after long and controversial discussions within the standardization bodies that reflected the differing backgrounds and intentions of the participants.

The first concrete idea of B-ISDN was simply to:

- add new high speed channels to the existing channel spectrum

- define new broadband user-network interfaces

- rely on existing 64 kbit/s ISDN protocols and only to modify or enhance them when absolutely unavoidable.

So in the dawn of B-ISDN, channel bit rates of 32...34 Mbit/s and around 45 Mbit/s, 70 Mbit/s and 135...139 Mbit/s were foreseen, and the corresponding channels were denominated H2, H3, H4.

These bit rates (and also the interface bit rate of about 140 Mbit/s) were oriented towards the bit rates of the plesiochronous hierarchy (CCITT Recommendation G.702 [32]), i.e. the H channels could have been transmitted within the signals of the corresponding hierarchical level. (The plesiochronous hierarchy is defined by a set of bit rates and multiplexing schemes for the multiplexing of several, not necessarily synchronous, 64 kbit/s ISDN channels into higher bit rate signals.)

These broadband channels would have provided a rigid bit rate scheme to be applied to all future broadband services which then were not yet fully described. This led to some concern about the suitability of the H channel concept.

Moreover, a decision regarding which and how many H and B channels should be incorporated into the broadband interface could not be achieved at all. There were proposals such as:

$$H4 + 4H1 + n \times B + \text{signalling channel} \qquad (\text{e.g. } n = 30)$$

to which a lot of critical questions were immediately raised:

- Is this the only interface option or will other channel combinations be allowed?

- Can the H4 channel be subdivided into smaller pieces (e.g. into $4 \times$ H2 or into B/H1/H2 combinations) or the 4 H1 channels be combined to yield a 6 Mbit/s or 8 Mbit/s entity?

- If several channel structures can be used as options at the interface, do they have to be fixed at subscription time or can they be dynamically changing?

These issues were never completely resolved since other ideas entered the discussion.

As another intermediate step, so-called hybrid interface structures were put forward comprising both channels for circuit-oriented (or stream) traffic and capacity to be used for burst-type traffic. Obviously, such structures would have been more flexible than merely channel-oriented ones.

Again, there were never-ending talks, now about where to draw the border between the stream and burst part of the interface, whether to allow it to change dynamically, and the steps in terms of bit rate by which changes could be made.

This deadlock situation was finally overcome by adopting an interface model based on a complete breakdown of its payload capacity into small pieces called *cells*, each of which may serve any purpose; i.e. each cell may be employed to carry information relating to whatever connection type.

In the following chapters this principle, embodied by the asynchronous transfer mode (ATM), and the impact on B-ISDN will be elaborated in more detail.

Chapter 2

B-ISDN Service Requirements

B-ISDN development can be justified and will be successful only if it meets the needs of potential future customers. Therefore, a brief outline of foreseeable broadband applications will be given before entering into a discussion of network aspects.

In principle, B-ISDN should be suitable for both business and residential customers, so besides all sorts of data communication, TV programme distribution and the provision of other entertainment facilities have to be considered.

B-ISDN will support services with both constant and variable bit rates, data, voice (sound), still and moving picture transmission, and of particular note, multi-media applications which may combine, say, data, voice and picture service components.

Some examples may be used to illustrate the capabilities of B-ISDN. In the business area, videoconferencing is already a well-established but still not commonly used method which facilitates the rapid exchange of information between people. As travelling can be avoided, videoconferencing helps to save time and costs. B-ISDN may considerably improve the current situation and allow videoconferencing to become a widespread telecommunication tool as it allows for high picture quality (at least today's TV quality or even better), which is crucial for the acceptance of videoconferencing by its users, and is able to provide connections between all potential users via standard interfaces.

Another salient feature of B-ISDN is the (cost-adequate) provision of high speed data links with flexible bit rate allocation for the interconnection of customer networks.

The residential B-ISDN user may appreciate the combined offer of text, graphics, sound, still images and films giving information about such things as holiday resorts, shops or cultural events.

Tables 2.1, 2.2, 2.3, 2.4 and 2.5 (based on [49]) give an overview of possible broadband services and applications as presented by CCITT.

7

Type of information	Examples of broadband services	Applications
Moving pictures and sound	Broadband video-telephony	Communication for the transfer of voice (sound), moving pictures, and video-scanned still images and documents between two locations (person-to-person) • Tele-education • Tele-shopping • Tele-advertising
	Broadband videoconference	Multipoint communication for the transfer of voice (sound), moving pictures, and video-scanned still images and documents between two or more locations (person-to-group, group-to-group) • Tele-education • Business conference • Tele-advertising
	Video-surveillance	• Building security • Traffic monitoring
	Video/audio information transmission service	• TV signal transfer • Video/audio dialogue • Contribution of information
Sound	Multiple sound-programme signals	• Multi-lingual commentary channels • Multiple programme transfers

Data	High speed unrestricted digital information transmission service	• High speed data transfer
		    LAN interconnection
		    MAN interconnection
		    Computer-computer interconnection
		• Transfer of video information
		• Transfer of other information types
		• Still image transfer
		• Multi-site interactive CAD/CAM

	High volume file transfer service	• Data file transfer
	High speed teleaction	• Real-time control • Telemetry • Alarms
Document	High speed telefax	User-to-user transfer of text, images, drawings, etc.
	High resolution image communication service	• Professional images • Medical images • Remote games
	Document communication service	User-to-user transfer of mixed documents*

*   Mixed document means that a document may contain text, graphics, still and moving picture information as well as voice annotation.

Table 2.1: *Conversational services*

Type of information	Examples of broadband services	Applications
Moving pictures (video) and sound	Video mail service	Electronic mailbox service for the transfer of moving pictures and accompanying sound
Document	Document mail service	Electronic mailbox service for mixed documents*

    *   Mixed document means that a document may contain text, graphics, still and moving picture information as well as voice annotation.

Table 2.2: *Messaging services*

Type of information	Examples of broadband services	Applications
Text, data, graphics, sound, still images, moving pictures	Broadband videotex	• Videotex including moving pictures • Remote education and training • Telesoftware • Tele-shopping • Tele-advertising • News retrieval
	Video retrieval service	• Entertainment purposes • Remote education and training
	High resolution image retrieval service	• Entertainment purposes • Remote education and training • Professional image communications • Medical image communications
	Document retrieval service	Mixed documents* retrieval from information centres, archives, etc.
	Data retrieval service	Telesoftware

    *   Mixed document means that a document may contain text, graphics, still and moving picture information as well as voice annotation.

Table 2.3: *Retrieval services*

Type of information	Examples of broadband services	Applications
Data	High speed unrestricted digital information distribution service	• Distribution of unrestricted data
Text, graphics, still images	Document distribution service	• Electronic newspaper • Electronic publishing
Moving pictures and sound	Video information distribution service	• Distribution of video/audio signals
Video	Existing quality TV distribution service (NTSC, PAL, SECAM)	TV programme distribution
	Extended quality TV distribution service • Enhanced definition TV distribution service • High quality TV	TV programme distribution
	High definition TV distribution service	TV programme distribution
	Pay-TV (pay-per-view, pay-per-channel)	TV programme distribution

Table 2.4: *Distribution services without user-individual presentation control*

Type of information	Examples of broadband services	Applications
Text, graphics, sound, still images	Full channel broadcast videography	• Remote education and training • Tele-advertising • News retrieval • Telesoftware

Table 2.5: *Distribution services with user-individual presentation control*

According to CCITT Recommendation I.211 [49], services are classified into *interactive* and *distribution* services. Interactive services comprise conversational, messaging and retrieval services; distribution services can be split into services with or without user-individual presentation control.

Conversational services can effect the mutual exchange of data, whole documents, pictures and sound. Examples are given in Table 2.1. B-ISDN messaging services include mailbox services for the transfer of sound, pictures and/or documents (Table 2.2). Retrieval services (Table 2.3) can be used, for example, to obtain video films at any time or to access a remote software library. Finally, some examples of distribution services (Tables 2.4 and 2.5) are electronic publishing and TV programme distribution with existing and, in the future, enhanced picture quality, e.g. high definition TV (HDTV).

To be able to derive, from assumed broadband services, the network requirements to be met by B-ISDN, [7] tried to compile technical characteristics of major B-ISDN applications. The results can be found in Table 2.6.

Service	Bit Rate (Mbit/s)	Burstiness
Data transmission (connection-oriented)	1.5 ... 130	1 - 50
Data transmission (connectionless)	1.5 ... 130	1
Document transfer/retrieval	1.5 ... 45	1 - 20
Videoconference/video-telephony	1.5 ... 130	1 - 5
Broadband videotex/video retrieval	1.5 ... 130	1 - 20
TV distribution	30 ... 130	1
HDTV distribution	130	1

Burstiness = peak bit rate/average bit rate

Table 2.6: *Characteristics of broadband services*

This table exhibits the following remarkable properties of broadband applications:

- Not all services require very high bit rates, but some do, especially moving picture services with high resolution. In Table 2.6, bit rates of 30 to 130 Mbit/s for TV distribution and 130 Mbit/s for HDTV distribution are given. Though these values may decrease in the future – e.g. there are ongoing activities to encode TV video signals with about 10 Mbit/s – the resulting bit rates will still be far above those employed for conventional ISDN services. The most demanding service will be HDTV which will consume at least a bit rate above 50 Mbit/s per HDTV channel.

- Several communication types are highly bursty in nature; if this feature was adequately reflected in network design, considerable economizing on network resources might be achieved (statistical multiplexing gain). In the case of TV and HDTV distribution the statistical multiplexing gain is hard to realize due to the nature of the source signals, therefore the burstiness is set to 1 in Table 2.6.

The variety of possible B-ISDN services and applications as shown here obviously requires a network with universal transfer capabilities to:

- cater for services which may employ quite different bit rates
- support burst-type traffic
- take into account both delay and loss-sensitive applications.

The network concept which is assumed to meet all these requirements will be presented in the following chapters.

Chapter 3

Principles and Building Blocks of B-ISDN

3.1 B-ISDN Principles

The motivation to incorporate broadband features into ISDN is neatly documented in CCITT Recommendation I.121 ('Broadband aspects of ISDN') [47]:

The B-ISDN recommendations were written taking into account the following:

- The emerging demand for broadband services (candidate services have been listed in the previous chapter).

- The availability of high speed transmission, switching and signal processing technologies (bit rates of hundreds of Mbit/s are being offered).

- The improved data and image processing capabilities available to the user.

- The advances in software application processing in the computer and telecommunication industries.

- The need to integrate interactive and distribution services and circuit and packet transfer modes into one universal broadband network. In comparison to several dedicated networks, service and network integration has major advantages in economic planning, development, implementation, operation and maintenance. While dedicated networks require several distinct and costly customer access lines, the B-ISDN access can be based on a single optical fibre for each customer. The large-scale production of highly integrated system components of a unique B-ISDN will lead to cost-effective solutions.

- The need to provide flexibility in satisfying the requirements of both user and operator (in terms of bit rate, quality of service etc.).

ISDN is conceived to support 'a wide range of audio, video and data applications in the same network' [47]. B-ISDN thus follows the same principles as 64 kbit/s

13

based ISDN (cf. CCITT Recommendation I.120 [46]) and is a natural extension of the latter [47]:

> *A key element of service integration is the provision of a wide range of services to a broad variety of users utilizing a limited set of connection types and multipurpose user-network interfaces.*

Whereas telecommunication networks of the pre-ISDN era have usually been specialized networks (e.g. for telephony or data) with rather limited bandwidth or throughput and processing capabilities, the future B-ISDN is conceived to become a universal (standardized) network supporting different kinds of applications and customer categories. CCITT Recommendation I.121 [47] presents an overview of B-ISDN capabilities:

> *B-ISDN supports switched, semi-permanent and permanent, point-to-point and point-to-multipoint connections and provides on demand, reserved and permanent services. Connections in B-ISDN support both circuit mode and packet mode services of a mono- and/or multi-media type and of a connectionless or connection-oriented nature and in a bidirectional or unidirectional configuration.*
> *A B-ISDN will contain intelligent capabilities for the purpose of providing advanced service characteristics, supporting powerful operation and maintenance tools, network control and management.*

We believe the reader of this list of intended B-ISDN capabilities must be deeply impressed; B-ISDN is tailored to become *the* universal future network!

B-ISDN implementations will, according to the CCITT, be based on the asynchronous transfer mode (ATM); this transfer mode will be briefly introduced in the next section (and its technical details will be discussed later, see Chapters 4 and 5).

3.2 Asynchronous Transfer Mode

The *asynchronous transfer mode* (ATM) is considered the ground on which B-ISDN is to be built [47]:

> *Asynchronous transfer mode (ATM) is the transfer mode for implementing B-ISDN ...*

The term *transfer* comprises both transmission and switching aspects, so a *transfer mode* is a specific way of transmitting and switching information in a network.

In ATM, all information to be transferred is packed into fixed-size slots called *cells*. These cells have a 48 octet information field and a 5 octet header. Whereas the information field is available for the user, the header field carries information that pertains to the ATM layer functionality itself, mainly the identification of cells by means of a label (see Figure 3.1).

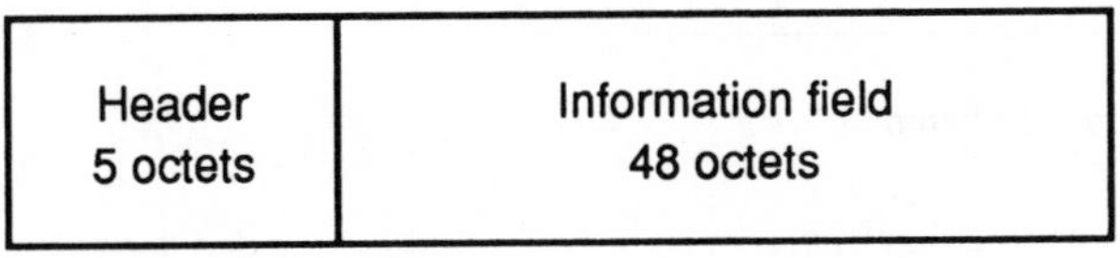

Header 5 octets	Information field 48 octets

Figure 3.1: *ATM cell structure*

A detailed description of the ATM layer functions and ATM header structure and coding will be given in Section 5.4. The protocol reference model for ATM-based networks will be addressed in Section 5.1; the boundaries between the ATM layer and other layers will be defined.

ATM allows the definition and recognition of individual communications by virtue of the label field inside each ATM cell header; in this respect, ATM resembles conventional packet transfer modes. Like packet switching techniques, ATM can provide a communication with a bit rate that is individually tailored to the actual need, including time-variant bit rates.

The term *asynchronous* in the name of the new transfer mode refers to the fact that, in the context of multiplexed transmission, cells allocated to the same connection may exhibit an irregular recurrence pattern as cells are filled according to the actual demand. This is shown in Figure 3.2(b).

In the *synchronous transfer mode* (STM) (see Figure 3.2(a)), a data unit associated with a given channel is identified by its position in the transmission frame, while in ATM (Figure 3.2(b)) a data unit or cell associated with a specific virtual channel may occur at essentially any position. The flexibility of bit rate allocation to a connection in STM is restricted due to predefined channel bit rates (e.g. B, H2; cf. Chapter 1) and the rigid structure of conventional transmission frames. These normally will not permit individual structuring of the payload or will only permit a quite limited selection of channel mixes at the corresponding interface at subscription time. Otherwise the network provider would have to manage a host of different interface types, a situation that the designer would try to avoid for obvious reasons (for example, STM switching of varying B and H channel mixes per interface requires switching equipment that can simultaneously handle all sorts of channels potentially used by customers at any time).

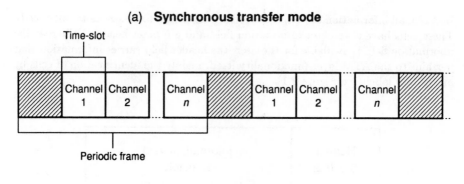

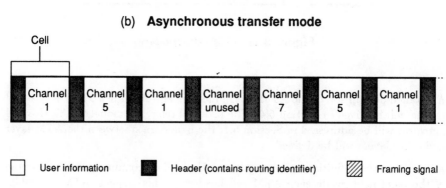

Figure 3.2: *STM and ATM principles*

In ATM-based networks the multiplexing and switching of cells is independent of the actual application. So the same piece of equipment in principle can handle a low bit rate connection as well as a high bit rate connection, be it of stream or burst nature. Dynamic bandwidth allocation on demand with a fine degree of granularity is provided. So the definition of high speed channel bit rates is now, in contrast to the situation in a STM environment, a second-rank task.

The flexibility of the ATM-based B-ISDN network access due to the cell transport concept strongly supports the idea of a unique interface which can be employed by a variety of customers with quite different service needs.

However, the ATM concept requires many new problems to be solved. For example, the impact of possible cell loss, cell transmission delay and cell delay variation on service quality needs to be determined (cf. Section 4.4). Other ATM-inherent difficulties – voice echo and tariffs – will be addressed in Sections 9.2 and 9.3.

To sum up, whereas today's networks are characterized by the coexistence of circuit switching and packet switching, B-ISDN will rely on a single, new method called ATM which combines advantageous features of both the circuit- and packet-oriented techniques. The former requires only low overhead and processing, and, once a circuit-switched connection is established, the transfer delay of the information being carried over it is low. The latter is much more flexible in terms of bit rate assigned to individual (virtual) connections. ATM is a circuit-oriented, hardware-controlled, low overhead concept of virtual channels which (by contrast with X.25 access [78]) have no flow control or error recovery. The implementation of these virtual channels is done by fixed-size (relatively short) cells and provides the basis for both switching and multiplexed transmission. The use of short cells in ATM and the high transfer rates involved (e.g. 150 Mbit/s, see Section 3.3) result in transfer delays and delay variations which are sufficiently small to enable universal applicability to a wide range of services including real-time services, e.g. voice and video. The capability of ATM to multiplex and switch on the cell level supports flexible bit rate allocation, as is known from packet networks.

The overall protocol architecture of ATM networks comprises:

- a single link-by-link cell transfer capability common to all services

- service-specific adaptation functions for mapping higher layer information into ATM cells on an end-to-end basis, e.g. packetization/depacketization of continuous bit streams into/from ATM cells or segmentation/reassembly of larger blocks of user information into/from ATM cells (core-and-edge concept).

Another important feature of ATM networks is the possibility of grouping several virtual channels into one so-called virtual path. The impact of this technique on the B-ISDN structure will be addressed in the following chapter.

3.3 Optical Transmission

The development of powerful and economic optical transmission equipment was the other big driving force for B-ISDN. Optical transmission is characterized by:

- low fibre attenuation (allowing for large repeater distances)

- high transmission bandwidths (up to several hundred Mbit/s)

- comparably small diameter (low weight/volume)

- high mechanical flexibility of the fibre

- resistance against electromagnetic fields

- low transmission error probability

- no cross-talk between fibres

- tapping much more difficult.

The high bandwidth of optical transmission systems – currently up to Gbit/s can be transported via one optical link – has led to early implementations in public networks to support existing services like telephony. Fibre-based local area networks are also widely in use nowadays, providing a bit rate in the order of magnitude of a hundred Mbit/s to the users.

So for B-ISDN the use of optical fibre-based transmission systems is straightforward from a technical viewpoint, at least in the trunk network and in the local access part of the network where considerable distances have to be bridged. (Technical details on optical transmission to be deployed in B-ISDNs will be discussed in Chapter 7.)

In B-ISDN at least about 150 Mbit/s will be offered to the user across the broadband user-network interface (cf. Section 5.2). Though much higher bit rates could comfortably be transmitted on optical fibre links, the costs of the electronics involved in the transmission equipment (e.g. sender/receiver in network terminations, terminals etc.) together with considerations on expected service needs – i.e. bit rates simultaneously required at the interface – led to the conclusion that a B-ISDN 'basic' interface at about 150 Mbit/s would be sufficient and adequate in many cases.

In addition, a second interface type with at least 600 Mbit/s in the direction from the network to the user is also foreseen (see Section 5.2). Handling of 600 Mbit/s ATM signals is still a challenge, the economic implementation of which is currently not so assured.

The deployment of highly reliable optical transmission systems with rather low bit error probabilities benefits a simplified network concept with, for example, potentially reducible data link layer functionality.

Chapter 4

B-ISDN Network Concept

4.1 General Architecture of the B-ISDN

The architectural model of the B-ISDN is described in CCITT Recommendation I.327 [53]. According to this recommendation, the information transfer and signalling capabilities of the B-ISDN comprise:

- broadband capabilities
- 64 kbit/s based ISDN capabilities
- user-to-network signalling
- inter-exchange signalling
- user-to-user signalling.

This is depicted in Figure 4.1.

Broadband information transfer is provided by ATM. The ATM data unit is the cell, a fixed-size block of 53 octets (cf. Section 5.4). The 5 octet cell header carries the necessary information to identify cells belonging to the same virtual channel. Cells are assigned on demand, depending on the source activity and the available resources.

ATM guarantees (under normal, i.e. fault-free, conditions) *cell sequence integrity.* This means that a cell belonging to a specific virtual channel connection can nowhere in the network overtake another cell of the same virtual channel connection that has been sent out earlier.

ATM is a connection-oriented technique. A connection within the ATM layer consists of one or more links, each of which is assigned an identifier. These identifiers remain unchanged for the duration of the connection.

Signalling information for a given connection is conveyed using a separate identifier (out-of-band signalling).

19

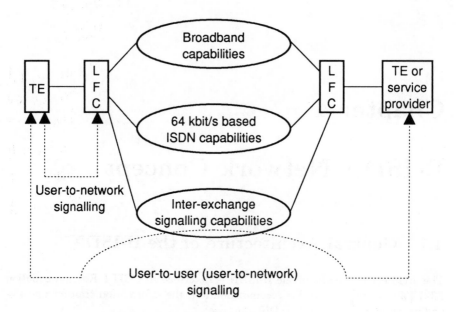

Figure 4.1: *Information transfer and signalling capabilities*

Though ATM is a connection-oriented technique, it offers a flexible transfer capability common to all services including connectionless data services. The proposed provision of connectionless data services via the ATM-based B-ISDN will be discussed later on in Section 9.1.

4.2   Networking Techniques

4.2.1   Network Layering

CCITT Recommendation I.311 [50] presents the layered structure of the B-ISDN depicted in Figure 4.2 (see also Section 5.1).

In this section, we only address the ATM transport network whose functions are split into two parts, namely physical layer transport functions and ATM layer transport functions.

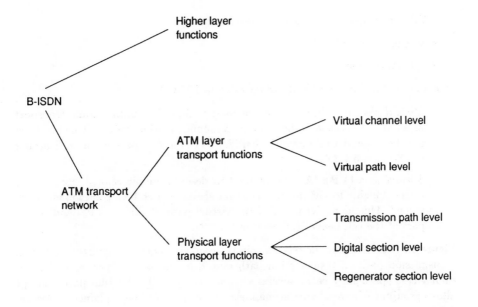

ATM   Asynchronous transfer mode

Figure 4.2: *B-ISDN layered structure*

Both the physical layer and the ATM layer are hierarchically structured. The physical layer consists of:

- transmission path level
- digital section level
- regenerator section level

which are defined in the following way:

> *Transmission path:* The transmission path extends between network elements that assemble and disassemble the payload of a transmission system (the payload will be used to carry user information; together with the necessary transmission overhead it forms the complete signal).

> *Digital section:* The digital section extends between network elements which assemble and disassemble continuous bit or byte streams.

> *Regenerator section:* The regenerator section is a portion of a digital section extending between two adjacent regenerators.

The ATM layer has two hierarchical levels, namely:

- virtual channel level
- virtual path level

which are defined in CCITT Recommendation I.113 [45]:

> *Virtual channel* (VC): 'A concept used to describe unidirectional transport of ATM cells associated by a common unique identifier value.' This identifier is called the virtual channel identifier (VCI) and is part of the cell header (cf. Section 5.4.2.4).

> *Virtual path* (VP): 'A concept used to describe unidirectional transport of cells belonging to virtual channels that are associated by a common identifier value.' This identifier is called the virtual path identifier (VPI) and is also part of the cell header (cf. Section 5.4.2.3).

Figure 4.3 demonstrates the relationship between virtual channel, virtual path and transmission path: a transmission path may comprise several virtual paths and each virtual path may carry several virtual channels. The virtual path concept allows grouping of several virtual channels. Its purpose will be explained in Section 4.2.3.

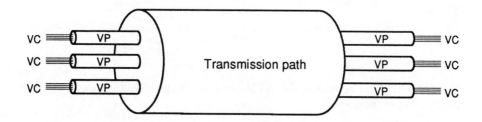

VC   Virtual channel
VP   Virtual path

Figure 4.3: *Relationship between virtual channel, virtual path and transmission path*

Concerning the levels of the ATM layer (virtual channel and virtual path), it proved helpful to distinguish between links and connections [45]:

- *Virtual channel link*: 'A means of unidirectional transport of ATM cells between a point where a VCI value is assigned and the point where that value is translated or removed.'

- Similarly, a *virtual path link* is terminated by the points where a VPI value is assigned and translated or removed.

A concatenation of VC links is called a *virtual channel connection* (VCC), and likewise, a concatenation of VP links is called a *virtual path connection* (VPC).

The relationship between different levels of the ATM transport network is demonstrated in Figure 4.4.

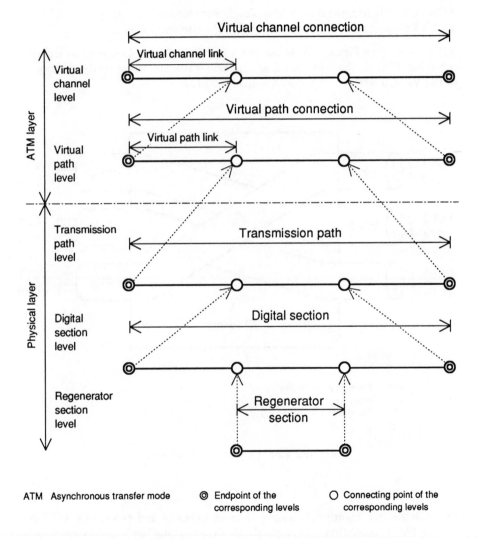

Figure 4.4: *Hierarchical layer-to-layer relationship*

A VCC may consist of several concatenated VC links, each of which is embedded in a VPC. The VPCs usually consist of several concatenated VP links. Each VP link is implemented on a transmission path which hierarchically comprises digital sections and regenerator sections.

4.2.2   Switching of Virtual Channels and Virtual Paths

VCIs and VPIs in general only have significance for one link. In a VCC/VPC the VCI/VPI value will be translated at VC/VP switching entities.

VP switches (see Figure 4.5) terminate VP links and therefore have to translate incoming VPIs to the corresponding outgoing VPIs according to the destination of the VP connection. VCI values remain unchanged.

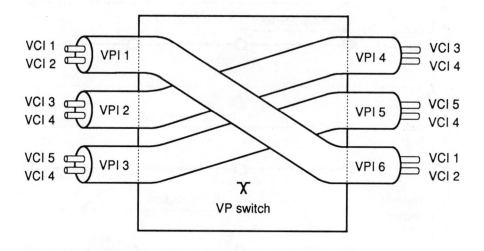

VCI	Virtual channel identifier
VP	Virtual path
VPI	Virtual path identifier

Figure 4.5: *Virtual path switching*

VC switches (see Figure 4.6) terminate both VC links and necessarily VP links. VPI and VCI translation is performed. As VC switching implies VP switching, in principle a VC switch can also handle mere VP switching.

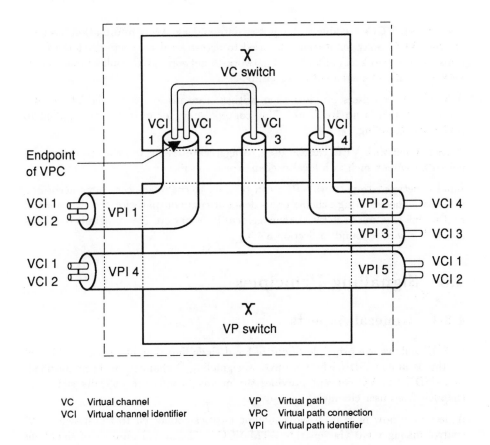

Figure 4.6: *Virtual channel/virtual path switching*

4.2.3 Applications of Virtual Channel/Path Connections

Virtual channel/path connections (VCCs/VPCs) can be employed between:

- user and user
- user and network
- network and network.

All cells associated with an individual VCC/VPC are transported along the same route through the network. Cell sequence is preserved (first sent - first received) for all VCCs.

User-to-user VCCs are able to carry user data and signalling information, user-to-network VCCs may for instance be used to access local connection related functions (user-network signalling), and network-to-network VCC applications include network traffic management and routing.

A VPC between users provides them with a transmission 'pipe' the VC organization of which is up to them. This concept may, for example, be applied to LAN-LAN coupling.

A user-to-network VPC can be used to aggregate traffic from a customer to a network element such as a local exchange or a specific server.

Finally, network-to-network VPCs can be used to organize user traffic according to a predefined routing scheme or to define a common path for the exchange of routing information or network management information. (More details on VCCs and VPCs can be found in Section 5.4.3.)

4.3   Signalling Principles

4.3.1   General Aspects

B-ISDN follows the principle of out-of-band signalling that has been established for the 64 kbit/s ISDN where a physical signalling D channel has been specified. In B-ISDN the VC concept provides the means to separate logically signalling channels from user channels.

A user may now have multiple signalling entities connected to the network call control management via separate ATM VCCs. The actual number of signalling connections and the bit rate allocated to them can be chosen in B-ISDN in a way that satisfies a customer's need optimally.

4.3.2   Capabilities Required for B-ISDN Signalling

B-ISDN signalling must be able to support:

- 64 kbit/s ISDN applications
- new broadband services.

This implies that existing signalling functions according to CCITT Recommendation Q.931 [74] must be included in B-ISDN signalling capabilities; on the other hand, the nature of B-ISDN – the ATM transport network – and the increasing desire for advanced communication forms like multi-media services require specific new signalling elements. In the following, an overview of necessary B-ISDN signalling capabilities is given. (More details on the implementation of such functions will be given in Section 5.6.2.)

ATM network-specific signalling capabilities have to be realized in order to:

- establish, maintain and release ATM VCCs and VPCs for information transfer

- negotiate (and perhaps renegotiate) the traffic characteristics of a connection.

Other signalling requirements are basically not ATM related but reflect the fact that more powerful service concepts appear. Examples are the support of multi-connection calls and multi-party calls.

For a multi-connection call, several connections have to be established to build up a 'composite' call comprising, for example, voice, image and data. It must also be possible to remove one or more connections of a call or to add new connections to the existing ones. A certain capability in the network to correlate the connections of a call is required. In any case, release of a call as a whole must be possible. These correlation functions should be performed in the origination and destination B-ISDN switch only, since the transit nodes should not be burdened with such tasks.

A multi-party call consists of several connections between more than two endpoints (conferencing). Signalling to indicate establishment/release of a multi-party call and adding/removing one party is required. (A communication that is part of a multi-party call may be of multi-connection nature itself.)

In a broadband environment, asymmetric connections (i.e. low or zero bandwidth in one direction and high bandwidth in the other) will gain relevance; signalling elements to support such connection types have to be established.

Another broadband issue impacting signalling is *interworking*, e.g. B-ISDN with non B-ISDN services, or between video services with different coding schemes.

4.3.3   Signalling Virtual Channels

In B-ISDN, signalling messages will be conveyed out-of-band in dedicated *signalling virtual channels* (SVCs). Different types of SVC are provided [50]; they are shown in Table 4.1.

There is one *meta-signalling virtual channel* (MSVC) per interface. This channel is bidirectional and permanent. It is a sort of interface management channel used to establish, check and release the point-to-point and selective broadcast SVCs.

Whereas the meta-signalling virtual channel is permanent, a point-to-point signalling channel is allocated to a signalling endpoint only while it is active.

A signalling endpoint at the user side may be located in a terminal or in the B-NT2 (e.g. private branch exchange). In a multi-functional terminal, multiple signalling endpoints may occur.

SVC Type	Directionality	Number of SVCs
Meta-signalling channel	Bidirectional	1
General broadcast SVC	Unidirectional	1
Selective broadcast SVC	Unidirectional	Several possible
Point-to-point SVC	Bidirectional	One per signalling endpoint

Table 4.1: *Signalling virtual channels at B-ISDN UNI*

The point-to-point signalling channels are bidirectional. They are used to establish, control and release VCCs or VPCs to carry user data (VPCs as well as VCCs may also be established without using signalling procedures, e.g. by subscription).

The broadcast SVCs are unidirectional (network-to-user direction only). They are used to send signalling messages either to all signalling endpoints in a customer's network or to a selected category of signalling endpoints. The general broadcast SVC reaches all signalling endpoints; it is implemented in any case. Selective broadcast SVCs may be provided in addition as a network option to be able to address all terminals belonging to the same service profile category (a B-ISDN service profile contains information which is maintained by the network to characterize the services offered by the network to the user; the service profile may be specified as in CCITT Recommendation Q.932, Annex A [75] or otherwise).

The provision of SVCs in the network is currently under discussion; so far no firm decisions have been taken but the principles outlined here are expected to apply.

To illustrate the SVC concept of B-ISDN, an example (based on CCITT Recommendation I. 311) is given in Figure 4.7, which highlights different possibilities for carrying signalling information from the customer to the network and vice versa.

Four different VP links/connections are depicted in the figure. The first (a) is a signalling VP link which transports all the signalling information to be exchanged between the customer and the local exchange, including meta-signalling. When a signalling capability to a point in the network other than the local exchange is required (e.g. in order to communicate with a special service provider located elsewhere), such signalling can be done on an extra VPC (c) which may carry signalling and user data. This VPC goes through the local exchange and is terminated at the appropriate place. (The other two VPs (b) and (d) shown for completeness in the figure carry user data only. In case (b) the corresponding VCs are switched in the local exchange and in case (d) the VP as a whole goes transparently through the local exchange.)

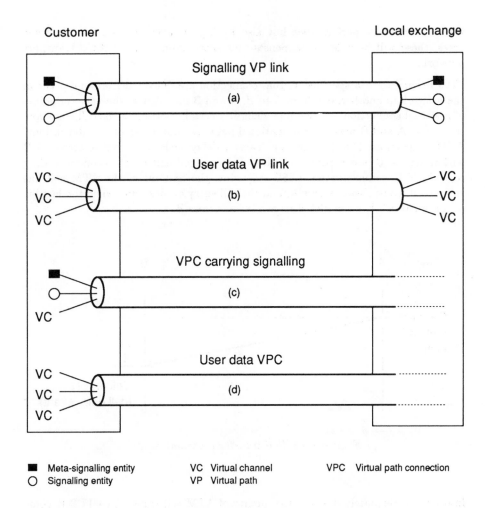

Figure 4.7: *Allocation of signalling virtual channels to a customer*

4.4   Broadband Network Performance

Broadband networks based on ATM cell transfer must meet certain performance requirements in order to be accepted by both potential users and network providers. ATM-related performance parameters and measures need to be specified in addition to the performance parameters already introduced for existing networks. In this section, we only deal with ATM layer-specific network performance. What the user will perceive as quality of service may be influenced not only by the ATM transport network performance but also by higher layer mechanisms. In some cases, these will be able to compensate for shortcomings in the ATM transport network.

Cells belonging to a specified virtual connection are delivered from one point in the network to another, e.g. from A to B. A and B may denote the very endpoints of a virtual connection, or they may delimit a certain portion of the cell transport route, e.g. A and B may indicate national network boundaries of an international ATM connection. Due to a certain transfer delay, cells sent from A arrive at B within $\Delta t > 0$ (see Figure 4.8). Note that the cell exit event occurs according to CCITT Recommendation I.35B [44] when the first bit of the ATM cell has completed transmission across A, and the cell entry event occurs when the last bit of the ATM cell has completed transmission across B.

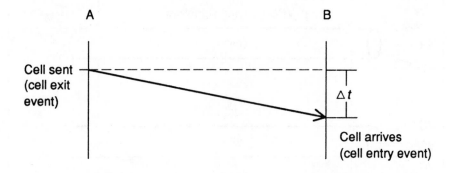

Figure 4.8: *Cell transfer (schematically)*

In order to adequately describe the quality of ATM cell transfer, CCITT Recommendation I.35B [44] first defines the following outcome categories:

- Successfully delivered cell
- Errored cell and severely errored cell
- Lost cell
- Inserted cell.

If Δt is less than a maximum allowed time T (the exact value is not yet specified), then the cell has been successfully delivered, otherwise a lost cell outcome occurs (i.e. either the cell arrives after T or it never reaches B). Errors in the VC/VP label field of the ATM cell header that cannot be corrected (cf. Section 5.3.1.5) or cell buffer overflows in the network (e.g. in an ATM switch) lead to lost cells.

If a cell arrives at B that has not been sent from A on this virtual connection, then such a misdelivered cell produces an inserted cell outcome. Label errors that are not detected or that are erroneously corrected may produce such inserted cells.

Successfully delivered cells arrive at their destination point in time but nevertheless may be errored when one or more bit errors exist in the cell information field. A cell is called severely errored when at least $N > 1$ bit errors occur in the cell information field with N yet to be specified (e.g. $N = 2$).

By making use of the above considerations, one can define the performance parameters. The parameters and their definitions are listed in Table 4.2.

Parameter	Definition
Cell loss ratio	Ratio of the number of lost cells to the sum of the number of lost and successfully delivered cells
Cell insertion rate	Number of inserted cells within a specified time interval (or per connection second)
Cell error ratio	Ratio of errored cells to the number of successfully delivered cells
Severely errored cell ratio	Ratio of the number of severely errored cells to the number of successfully delivered cells
Cell transfer delay	Δt (see Figure 4.8)
• Mean cell transfer delay	Arithmetic average of a specified number of cell transfer delays
• Cell delay variation	Difference between a single observation of cell transfer delay and the mean cell transfer delay on the same connection
Cell transfer capacity	The maximum possible number of successfully delivered cell outcomes occurring over a specified ATM connection during a unit of time

Table 4.2: *ATM performance parameters*

Note that in Table 4.2 cell loss and cell error *ratios* are given whereas the cell insertion outcomes are measured by a *rate* (i.e. events per time unit). As the mechanism by which inserted cells are produced has nothing to do with the number of cells on the observed connection, this performance parameter cannot be expressed as a ratio, only as a rate.

Bit errors in errored cells can be corrected to a certain extent by error protection methods applied to the cell information field contents (see Section 5.5).

Lost and inserted cells can cause severe trouble in the event that they are not

detected; e.g. for constant bit rate, the real-time services synchronism between
sending and receiving terminals may be disturbed. Lost and inserted cell events
become detectable (in many cases) by the supervision of a sequence number in the
cell information field or an equivalent mechanism (see Section 5.5).

Both cell transfer delay and cell delay variation must be kept within a limited
range in order to meet service requirements. Cell delay and delay variation are
induced, for example, by ATM multiplexers or ATM switches (see Chapters 6 and
7).

ATM network performance requirements in terms of parameter values are not
specified yet; this issue will be addressed again, however, in the following chapters
whenever appropriate (e.g. in Chapters 6 and 7 on ATM switching and transmission).

4.5   Traffic Control and Resource Management

4.5.1   Overview of Traffic Control Functions

To ensure the desired broadband network performance outlined in the previous
section, an ATM-based network will have to provide a set of traffic control capabilities. CCITT Recommendation I.311 [50] identifies the following:

- Connection admission control

- Usage parameter control

- Priority control

- Congestion control.

Their definition and description are given in the subsequent sections.

4.5.1.1   Connection Admission Control

Connection admission control is defined as 'the set of actions taken by the network
at the call set-up phase (or during call renegotiation phase) in order to establish
whether a (VC/VP) connection can be accepted' [50].

A connection can only be accepted if sufficient network resources are available
to establish the connection end to end at its required quality of service. The
agreed quality of service of already existing connections in the network must not
be influenced by the new connection.

Two classes of parameters are foreseen to support connection admission control:

- A set of parameters describing the source traffic characteristics.

- Another set of parameters to identify the required quality of service class.

Source traffic can be characterized by its:

- average bit rate
- peak bit rate
- burstiness
- peak duration.

The exact definition of burstiness and peak duration is still a pending issue in CCITT (burstiness might be defined as the ratio of peak bit rate to average bit rate). The description of source traffic parameters and quality of service class parameters cannot be completed unless more profound knowledge about ATM service requirements is compiled.

4.5.1.2 Usage Parameter Control

Usage parameter control is defined as 'the set of actions taken by the network to monitor and control user traffic in terms of traffic volume and cell routing validity. Its main purpose is to protect network resources from *malicious* as well as *unintentional misbehaviour* which can affect the quality of service of other already established connections by detecting violations of negotiated parameters. Usage parameter control will apply only during the information transfer phase of a connection. Connection monitoring encompasses all connections crossing the user-network interface, including signalling' [50].

Usage parameter monitoring includes the following functions:

- Checking of the validity of VPI/VCI values
- Monitoring the traffic volume entering the network from active VP and VC connections in order to ensure that parameters agreed upon are not violated
- Monitoring the total volume of the accepted traffic on the access link.

What is actually performed will depend on the access network configuration.

The parameters subject to monitoring and control may be the same as those used for source traffic characterization to support connection admission control, namely average and peak bit rate, burstiness and peak duration. However, further studies are required.

Usage parameter control can simply *discard* those cells which violate the negotiated traffic parameters. In addition, a 'guilty' connection may be released. Another, less rigorous option would be *tagging* of violating cells. These cells can be transferred as long as they do not cause any serious harm to the network. Thus the overall throughput of ATM cells might possibly be raised.

To illustrate the concept of usage parameter control, Figure 4.9 shows different access network arrangements with the appropriate usage parameter control measures applied to VCs or VPs at the access point where they are terminated within the network.

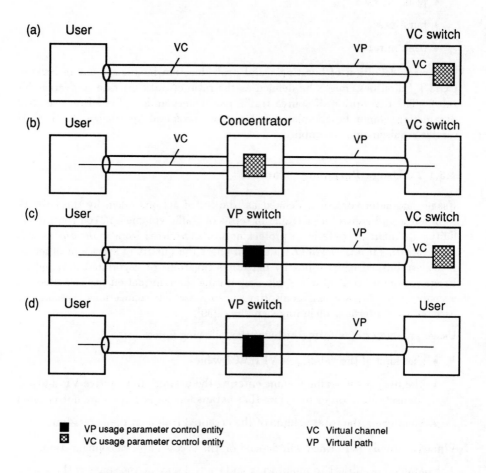

Figure 4.9: *Illustration of usage parameter control*

In case (a), a user is connected directly to a VC switch. Usage parameter control is performed within the VC switch on VCs before switching them.

In case (b), a user is connected to a VC switch via a concentrator. Usage parameter control is performed within the concentrator on VCs only.

In case (c), a user is connected to a VC switch via a VP switch. Here usage parameter control is performed within the VP switch on VPs only and within the VC switch on VCs only.

In case (d), a user is connected to another user via a VP switch. Usage parameter control is now performed within the VP switch on VPs only.

Usage parameter control principles may also be applied to control the volume of traffic coming from other networks at the entry of an ATM-based network (from the ATM network's viewpoint, the other network is considered a big user). This so-called *inter-network usage parameter control* merits further study.

4.5.1.3 Priority Control

ATM cells have an explicit cell loss priority bit in the header (see Section 5.4.2.7), so two different ATM priority classes can be distinguished. A single ATM connection (on virtual path or channel level) can comprise both priority classes when the information to be transmitted is classified by the user into more and less important parts (one possible application may be layered video-coding). In this case the two priority classes could be treated separately by connection admission control and usage parameter control.

The details of this priority control and the need for additional priority mechanisms are still an open issue.

In [117] different buffering mechanisms for systems with two priorities are described:

> *Common buffer with pushout mechanism*: Cells of both priorities share a common buffer. If the buffer is full and a high priority cell arrives, a cell with low priority (if any is available) will be pushed out and lost. In order to guarantee the cell sequence integrity, a complicated buffer management mechanism is necessary.

> *Partial buffer sharing*: Low priority cells can only access the buffer if the total buffer filling is less than a given threshold S_L (S_L < total buffer capacity). High priority cells can access the whole buffer. By adjusting the threshold S_L it is possible to adapt the system to various load situations.

> *Buffer separation*: For the two priorities, different buffers are used. This mechanism is simple to implement but cell sequence integrity can only be maintained if a single priority is assigned to each connection.

The results given in [117] showed that the system performance can be improved using priorities and that the *partial buffer sharing* mechanism is a very good strategy (best compromise between performance and implementation).

4.5.1.4   Congestion Control

Congestion in the context of B-ISDN is defined as 'a state of network elements (e.g. switches, concentrators, transmission links) in which, due to traffic overload and/or control resource overload, the network is not able to guarantee the negotiated quality of service to the already established connections and to the new connection requests' [50]. Congestion can be caused by unpredictable statistical fluctuations of traffic flows or fault conditions within the network.

Congestion control is a network means of minimizing congestion effects and avoiding the congestion state spreading. Congestion control can employ connection admission and/or usage parameter control procedures to avoid overload situations. For example, congestion control could reduce the peak bit rate available to a user and monitor this (and react accordingly if the user exceeds the new parameter value).

Another congestion control procedure is called *fast reservation protocol* [19]. It is claimed to allow an *intelligent* multiplexing of sporadic and variable bit rate sources both without real-time requirements. When using such a procedure, cell losses caused by the statistical behaviour of the individual traffic streams can be reduced.

4.5.2   Traffic Control Procedures and Their Impact on Resource Management

Traffic control procedures for ATM networks are currently not standardized within CCITT. In fact, it has not been decided yet whether, and to what extent, they should be standardized at all. On the one side, network providers may have a desire for flexible network tools to be able to react adequately to customers' needs (which speaks against standardization), while on the other side, for the benefit of users and especially terminal manufacturers, settled network standards are indispensable. For instance, a terminal basically needs to know how the network handles its ATM cells under normal and also fault conditions in order to shape its cell flow according to the rules of the ATM network and thus to be able to use the transport facilities of the ATM network optimally.

The choice of traffic control algorithms directly impacts on a network's resource allocation strategy. For example, if only the peak bit rate of a connection were considered for admission and usage parameter control, then this peak bit rate would have to be allocated to the connection. If this connection had a low average bit rate, then most of the time the network would exhibit a quite poor efficiency. Nevertheless, such simple strategies can assist in quickly introducing ATM-based networks; as long as knowledge about the management of ATM traffic flows is rather limited, due to the fact that neither the source traffic characteristics nor the actual traffic mixes on a link are sufficiently clear, it might be wise to stay on safe ground even if a considerable amount of network capacity is wasted. Besides peak bit rate reservation, a restricted utilization (e.g. 70 %) of the cell transport capability of a link helps to avoid congestion.

The goal is simultaneously to:

- achieve good ATM network efficiency
- meet the users' quality of service requirements

with a method that is generally applicable. Therefore, more sophisticated traffic control measures and resource management actions are being taken into account.

One example of a complex connection admission and bandwidth allocation algorithm is given in [103]. In this approach, both average and peak bit rate are considered and, in addition, the upper bound for the bit rate variance that is dependent on the behaviour of the source (a good representation of the bit rate variance is especially important when the source is a video codec). The results are promising: this method has a considerable advantage compared with mere peak bit rate reservation if the peak bit rates of most of the connections on a link are small in relation to the total bit rate of the link and if the peak-to-average bit rate ratio (burstiness) of these connections is high.

Different usage parameter control mechanisms have been proposed, namely *leaky bucket, sliding window, jumping window* and *exponentially weighted moving average*. Their modelling and their performance are presented in [134]. The comparison of these mechanisms showed that the leaky bucket and the exponentially weighted moving average are most promising with respect to flexibility and implementation complexity.

The basic problem of ATM networks is the statistical behaviour of the cell arrival process, e.g. at a buffer where cells generated by several sources are multiplexed together.

The ATM traffic can be described by a three-level hierarchical model as depicted in Figure 4.10 [107, 137].

The call level has a typical time scale of seconds up to hours, the burst level is related with the millisecond range up to seconds, and the cell level with the microsecond range. These levels have different impacts on network implementation: whereas cell level analysis can provide information for buffer dimensioning (e.g. in ATM switches or multiplexers), the burst level characteristics influence mainly call admission strategies, and the call level considerations relate to ATM link dimensioning.

Based on the traffic model shown in Figure 4.10, mathematical models have been defined with different levels of abstraction [118] including:

- burstiness (peak bit rate/average bit rate)
- geometrically distributed burst lengths

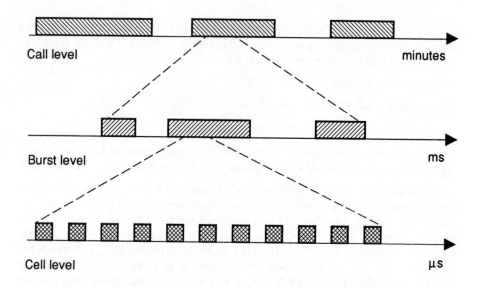

Figure 4.10: *Hierarchical modelling of ATM traffic*

- switched Poisson process
- Markov-modulated Poisson process
- generally modulated deterministic process.

It has been found that the quality of service parameters (e.g. jitter, loss probability) are very sensitive to the assumed source characteristic. Therefore, it is necessary that, for performance evaluation, these detailed source traffic models are used.

4.6   Operation and Maintenance Aspects

4.6.1   General Principles

CCITT Recommendation M.60 [68] defines *maintenance* as:

> *The combination of all technical and corresponding administrative actions, including supervision actions, intended to retain an item in, or restore it to, a state in which it can perform a required function.*

The general principles for the maintenance of telecommunication networks relevant also to B-ISDN are contained in CCITT Recommendation M.20 ('Maintenance philosophy for telecommunications networks') [65] and CCITT Recommendation M.36 ('Principles for the maintenance of ISDNs') [67].

Table 4.3 gives a brief overview of operation and maintenance (OAM) actions (cf. CCITT Recommendations M.20 [65] and I.610 [64]).

Action	Description
Performance monitoring	Normal function of the managed entity is monitored by the continuous or periodic checking of functions. As a result, maintenance event information will be produced.
Defect and failure detection	Malfunctions or predicted malfunctions are detected by continuous or periodic checking. As a result, maintenance event information or various alarms will be produced.
System protection	Effect of failure of managed entity is minimized by blocking or change-over to other entities. As a result, the failed entity is excluded from operation.
Failure or performance information	Failure information is given to other management entities. As a result, alarm indications are given to other management planes. Response to a status report request will also be given.
Fault localization	Determination by internal or external test systems of failed entity if failure information is insufficient.

Table 4.3: *Overview of OAM actions*

Another recommendation relevant to OAM of B-ISDN is CCITT Recommendation M.30 [66] entitled 'Principles for a telecommunications management network' (TMN). An example of TMN architecture for the B-ISDN customer access will be given in Section 5.7.

4.6.2   OAM Levels in B-ISDN

The OAM levels of the ATM transport network coincide with the levels introduced in Section 4.2.1 on network layering (see Figures 4.2 and 4.4): the ATM transport network comprises the physical layer and the ATM layer, and these layers are subdivided into regenerator section, digital section and transmission path level, and virtual path and virtual channel level (cf. Figure 4.11).

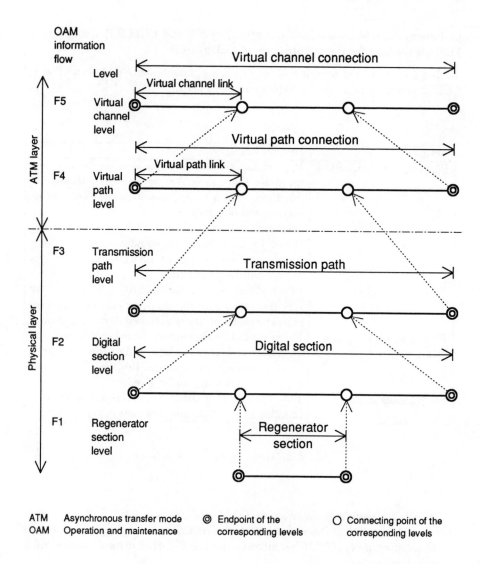

Figure 4.11: *OAM hierarchical levels*

The corresponding OAM information flows of each level – denominated F1 to F5 – are also depicted in Figure 4.11.

The OAM flows are bidirectional. As an example of an OAM flow, consider the monitoring of a VPC by means of monitoring cells sent out at one endpoint of the VPC and mirrored at the other endpoint, to be evaluated at the sending side.

In Section 5.7, more information on these OAM information flows relating to the user-to-network access is presented.

4.7 Customer Network Aspects

One essential block of the B-ISDN is the *customer network* (CN). Sometimes it is called *customer premises network* (CPN) or *subscriber premises network* (SPN).

4.7.1 Reference Configuration of the B-ISDN UNI

The reference configuration for the 64 kbit/s ISDN user-network interface (UNI), which is described in CCITT Recommendation I.411 [57], was accepted to be general enough also for application in the B-ISDN environment [59]. Figure 4.12 shows the principles of the reference configuration for the B-ISDN UNI. It contains the following:

- Functional groups: B-NT1, B-NT2 and B-TE1
- Reference points : T_B and S_B

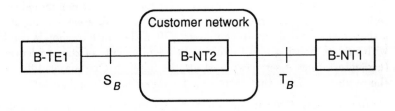

| B-NT | Network termination for B-ISDN |
| B-TE | Terminal equipment for B-ISDN |

Figure 4.12: *Reference configuration of the B-ISDN UNI*

B-NT1 and B-NT2 are generic terms and denote broadband network terminations. B-TE1 is the acronym for a broadband terminal with standard interface. At the reference points T_B and S_B, physical interfaces may or may not occur. If they are realized, they must comply with the specified standard (see Section 5.2). While the B-NT1 performs only line transmission termination and related OAM functions, the B-NT2 may be, for example, a private branch exchange or LAN which performs multiplexing and switching of ATM cells.

The CN covers the area where users have access to the public network via their terminals. This is the part of the telecommunication network located at the user side of the B-NT1.

For the functional description of the CN, the reference configuration shown in Figure 4.12 can be used. The interface between the CN and the public network is usually at the reference point T_B. So the CN coincides with the functional group B-NT2 (see Figure 4.12).

4.7.2   Customer Categories

Different aspects for the classification of CNs are possible [9, 14, 86], e.g. environment (residential, business), number of users or topology.

The *residential* environment is characterized by a small number of people (e.g. a family) using broadband services mainly for entertainment purposes. This category is considered to be more or less homogeneous and will be restricted to one flat or house. In many cases, no internal switching capabilities are necessary within a residential CN.

The counterpart of the residential CNs are the *business* CNs which are subdivided according to their size:

Small business CNs: Small business CNs have a lot of commonality with residential CNs. Such a CN will be installed in small areas like an office or a shop with up to about 10 employees. Often the office or shop is combined with private housing and therefore the requirements of the residential CN (e.g. entertainment services) must also be fulfilled. One major difference to the residential CN is that there may be a need for internal switching.

Medium business CNs: In medium and large business CNs, as well as factory CNs, no distribution service for entertainment purposes need be supported. Normally, only interactive services, e.g. telephony, videoconference or high speed data transmission, will be used. One of the main characteristics is the internal switching capability. A medium business CN has typically between 10 and 100 users.

Large business CNs: Large business CNs have more than 100 users. They spread over several buildings or floors of a building. Sometimes distances of up to 10 km must be spanned.

Factory CNs: Factory CNs can have the size of a medium or large business CN. They often have to satisfy exceptional physical requirements such as being robust against extraordinary heat, dust or electromagnetic interference.

The common characteristic feature of the medium, large and factory CNs is the provision of internal communication. This facility is not so often required in the residential and small business environment.

4.7.3 General Requirements

Two types of requirements are expected to be met by a CN [144]:

- Service requirements
- Structural requirements.

Service requirements deal with the service mix as well as the consequences of having to support these services. The service mix is dependent on the customer categories. This type of requirement includes the bit rate to be supported, the information transfer characteristics like mean and maximum delay, delay variation, error performance and throughput. It is possible to characterize realistic service mixes for each of the customer categories, but it is rather difficult to estimate the evolution of coding techniques (e.g. variable bit rate video-coding) which influence the required bit rate of a specific service.

The second type of requirements are called *structural requirements* which include aspects of flexibility, modularity, reliability, physical performance and cost.

Flexibility of the CN is the ability to cope with system changes. This can be subdivided into four parts:

1. *Adaptability* is the requirement which measures how the CN deals with changes that do not alter the global scale of the CN (e.g. new wiring). This is very important in the terminal area for the residential as well as the business environment.

2. *Expandability* indicates how the CN can grow (e.g. introduction of new services, increasing the bit rate to be supported, or installation of new terminals, expanding the scale of the CN).

3. *Mobility* is the ability of interchanging terminals. This requires a universal terminal interface.

4. *Interworking* describes how the CN can interface to other networks. This is very important in areas which are already covered by existing networks (e.g. LAN, private MAN).

Modularity is the provision of a flexible structure. The network should not be limited to a few applications. Therefore, it is necessary that a modular system is used for the provision of CN capabilities.

Reliability deals with the sensitivity of the CN to errors (e.g. bit errors, terminal failures and user-induced errors). This requirement is extremely important when a large number of people or terminals are afflicted by the error or in all cases where a very good operation of the CN must be guaranteed (e.g. hospitals or fire departments). Reliability requires redundancy and therefore within large CNs even the terminal connection is duplicated.

Physical performance concerns the optimum use of the physical medium. It includes aspects of coding efficiency and cable length and influences the hardware cost. Installation and maintenance are covered by the operating performance. This must be very simple in the terminal environment so that changes can be carried out rapidly and cheaply.

Cost is one of the most important requirements influencing the acceptance of the CN. In the residential area, low costs are essential whereas in the business area it is necessary to have reasonable costs during the introduction phase. Fast system growth can only be achieved if the incremental costs can be kept low.

4.7.4 Topologies

In CCITT Recommendation I.413 different physical configurations for the realization of a CN are illustrated [59]. Figure 4.13 shows a few examples for CN configurations. (Other CN configurations are not precluded.)

The first configuration is the well-known star configuration where each terminal is directly connected to the B-NT2 by its dedicated line.

A B-NT2 can be realized as a centralized system or a distributed system. Such a distributed system can have LAN-like structures (e.g. bus or ring) where the terminals are all connected to a common medium via special medium adaptors in the general case.

But CCITT also agreed to some new configurations where terminals are directly connected to a common shared medium (e.g. dual bus) as shown in Figure 4.13(b) and (c). The major motivations for these new configurations are simplification of deployment, reasons of economy and evolutionary aspects of B-ISDN [88]. The extension of a shared medium configuration can be achieved easily by adding a new terminal. When using a star configuration, extension may result in higher costs caused by an additional or larger multiplexer.

Combinations of the star configuration and the shared medium configurations are also possible (see Figure 4.13(c)). The configuration depicted in this figure shows the starred bus system.

It is evident that terminals used in the shared medium configurations of Figure 4.13 have to include a medium access function. This can be supported by the generic flow control (GFC) protocol of the ATM layer (see Section 5.4.2.2). The GFC mechanism provides orderly and fair access of terminals to the shared medium by supervising the cell streams and assigning capacity to contending terminals on a per-cell basis.

The influence of these new configurations on the definition of the interface between a terminal and the B-NT2 will be discussed in Section 5.2.

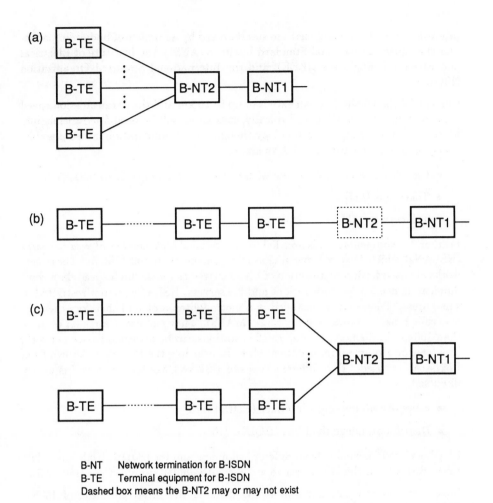

B-NT   Network termination for B-ISDN
B-TE   Terminal equipment for B-ISDN
Dashed box means the B-NT2 may or may not exist

Figure 4.13: *Physical configurations of the CN*

4.7.5   Interworking with Existing Networks

In the medium and large business environments, two different types of communication system are presently used: voice and facsimile communication are handled by *private branch exchanges* (PBXes) whereas the need for high speed data communication is satisfied by LANs.

The number of LANs used within business premises has dramatically increased in the last few years. There are a number of protocols available that have different

principles of operation and that are standardized by a number of bodies, in particular the American National Standard Institute (ANSI), the Institute of Electrical
and Electronic Engineers (IEEE), and the International Standard Organization
(ISO).

Current LANs usually have an extent of up to 10 km and their transmission speed
is in the range 1 - 16 Mbit/s. Typically, coax cable will be used for transmission.
Most LANs use a ring or bus topology though a star configuration is also possible.
Today's most frequently used LANs are:

- Carrier sense multiple access with collision detection (CSMA/CD) [110]
- Token bus [111]
- Token ring [112].

Further developments in this area led to the so-called *high speed local area networks*
(HSLANs) which have a transmission rate of more than 100 Mbit/s. These networks are used for interconnection of LANs as well as for the high speed data communication needed by workstations and file-servers. HSLANs are not restricted to
small areas. They may be installed in a metropolitan area and therefore they are
also called *metropolitan area networks* (MANs). They can cover a region of more
than 100 km in diameter and up to 1000 stations can be attached to one network.
The transmission medium is optical fibre. In principle the topologies known from
LANs can be used. Two different types of HSLANs/MANs are most frequently
discussed:

- Fibre-distributed data interface (FDDI) [113]
- Distributed queue dual bus (DQDB) [108].

FDDI is already available from different suppliers and for DQDB, trials and pilots
exist. HSLANs in the Gbit/s range are currently under study (cf. Section 10.5).

Increasing communication requirements demand the interconnection of LANs.
This can be achieved by the use of MANs as well as B-ISDN. Therefore, it is
necessary to interconnect LANs and private MANs with B-ISDN. For that purpose, an *interworking unit* (IWU) will be used. This IWU can be attached directly
to the B-NT1, as shown in Figure 4.14(a), or the LAN/MAN can be connected by
means of the IWU via S_B to a B-NT2 if present, as shown in Figure 4.14(b).

The IWU may become a bottleneck in the case of heavy traffic load. To obtain a
good performance (e.g. high throughput, small delay) it is necessary that the protocols used in the LAN and in B-ISDN have a lot of commonality. Interconnection
should be done on the lowest possible level. With today's protocols, this can only
be achieved by the interconnection of DQDB with B-ISDN. Further details of the
LAN/MAN integration into B-ISDN will be presented in Section 8.4.

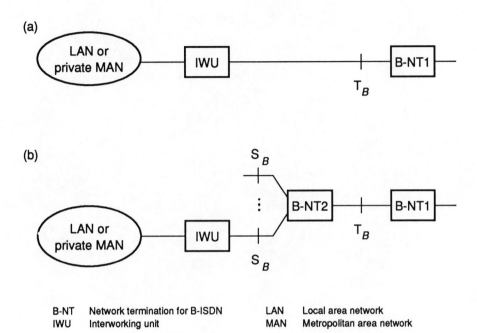

B-NT	Network termination for B-ISDN	LAN	Local area network
IWU	Interworking unit	MAN	Metropolitan area network

Figure 4.14: *Interworking LAN - B-ISDN*

Chapter 5

B-ISDN User-Network Interfaces and Protocols

This chapter deals with the B-ISDN user-network interfaces and with ATM-based protocols. In Section 5.1 the protocol reference model developed by CCITT for B-ISDN is presented. The next sections, Sections 5.2 and 5.3, describe the user-network interfaces in general and their physical layer properties. Then in the following sections, Sections 5.4 and 5.5, functions, codings and procedures of the adjacent ATM layer and ATM adaptation layer are described. Higher layer aspects of both user plane and control plane (signalling) are described in Section 5.6. A section on operation and maintenance problems of the user-network interfaces (Section 5.7) concludes Chapter 5.

5.1   B-ISDN Protocol Reference Model

5.1.1   General Aspects

In modern communication systems, a layered approach is used for the organization of all communication functions. The functions of the layers and the relations of the layers with respect to each other are described in a *protocol reference model* (PRM).

A description of the PRM for the existing ISDN is given in CCITT Recommendation I.320 [51]. In particular it has introduced the concept of separated planes for the segregation of user, control and management functions. This PRM is the basis for the PRM of the broadband aspects of ISDN (B-ISDN PRM) which is described in CCITT Recommendation I.321 [52]. The new recommendation has the purpose of taking into account the functionalities of B-ISDN. Therefore, expansions of the PRM contained in CCITT Recommendation I.320 were necessary.

49

5.1.2   Layered Architecture

According to the reference model of *open system interconnection* (OSI) of the ISO [109] each open system can be described as a set of subsystems arranged in a vertical sequence (see Figure 5.1).

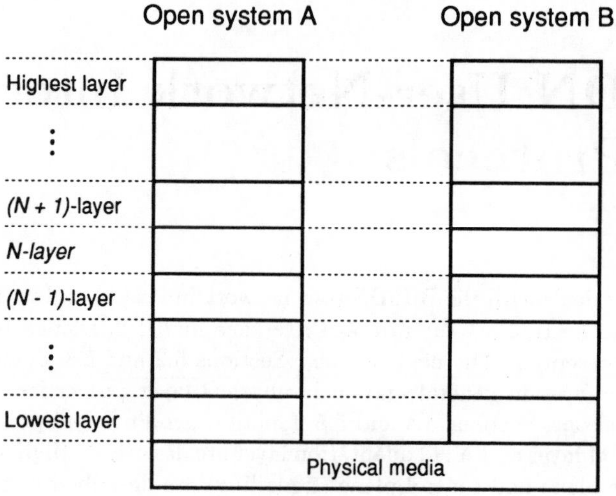

Figure 5.1: *Layered structure of the OSI reference model*

An N-subsystem which consists of one or more N-entities only interacts with the subsystem above or below. The N-entity performs functions within layer N. For the communication between peer N-entities (entities of layer N) an N-peer-to-peer protocol will be used. The unit of data in an N-peer-to-peer protocol is called the N-protocol data unit (N-PDU). Peer N-entities communicate using the services provided by the layer below. The services of layer N are provided to layer $(N+1)$. The point at which the N-services can be accessed by the layer above is called the N-service access point (N-SAP).

For a description of the interface between the adjacent layers N and $(N + 1)$ the N-primitives are introduced. Together with the N-primitive the associated N-service data unit (N-SDU) is delivered from layer N to layer $(N + 1)$ and vice versa. For this purpose the N-service protocol (adjacent layer protocol) is used. Figure 5.2 presents this service concept.

In Figure 5.3 the relationships among the various types of data units are shown. An N-PDU consists of an N-protocol control information (N-PCI) and an N-user data. The N-PCI is the information which is exchanged between N-entities.

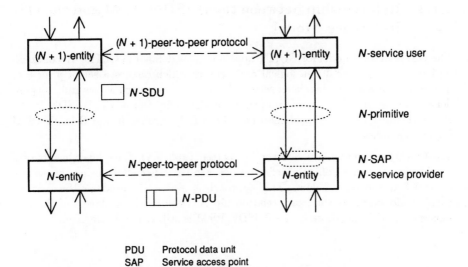

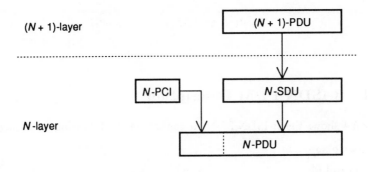

PDU   Protocol data unit
SAP   Service access point
SDU   Service data unit

Figure 5.2: *OSI service concept*

PCI   Protocol control information
PDU   Protocol data unit
SDU   Service data unit

Figure 5.3: *Relationships among the various types of data units*

5.1.3   Relationship between the B-ISDN PRM and the OSI Reference Model

The OSI reference model for CCITT applications is defined in CCITT Recommendation X.200 [80]. OSI is a logical architecture which defines a set of principles including protocol layering, layer service definition, service primitives and independence. These principles are appropriate for the definition of the B-ISDN PRM. However, not all of these principles have been fully applied in the B-ISDN PRM (e.g. independence).

The OSI reference model uses seven layers (see Table 5.1). Each layer has its own specific functions and offers a defined service to the layer above using the service provided by the layer below. This approach is also well suited for the B-ISDN PRM. Unfortunately, the exact relationship between the lower layers of the OSI reference model and those of the B-ISDN PRM is still not fully clarified.

Layer	Name
7	Application layer
6	Presentation layer
5	Session layer
4	Transport layer
3	Network layer
2	Data link layer
1	Physical layer

Table 5.1: *OSI reference model*

5.1.4   B-ISDN PRM Description

Figure 5.4 shows the B-ISDN PRM. It consists of the following three planes:

- User plane
- Control plane
- Management plane.

The *management plane* includes two types of functions called *layer management* functions and *plane management* functions. All the management functions which relate to the whole system are located in the plane management. Its task is to provide coordination between all planes. No layered structure is used within this plane.

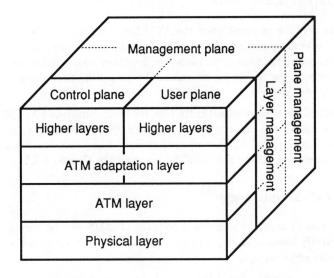

ATM   Asynchronous transfer mode

Figure 5.4: *B-ISDN protocol reference model*

The *layer management* has a layered structure. It performs the management functions relating to resources and parameters residing in its protocol entities (e.g. meta-signalling). For each layer the layer management handles the specific OAM information flows. More details about these management functions are presented in CCITT Recommendation Q.940 [76].

The *user plane* provides for the transfer of user information. All associated mechanisms like flow control or recovery from errors are included. A layered approach is used within the user plane.

Within the *control plane* a layered structure is also used. This plane is responsible for call control and connection control functions. These are all signalling functions which are necessary to set up, supervise and release a call or a connection.

The functions of the physical layer (PL) and the ATM layer are the same for the control plane and the user plane. Different functions may occur in the ATM adaptation layer (AAL) as well as in higher layers.

5.1.5   Layer Functions

The functions of the physical layer, the ATM layer and the ATM adaptation layer, the primitives exchanged between layers, and the primitives exchanged between these layers and the management plane are described in the following subsections. The functions of the higher layers cannot be presented here because at present they are not well defined.

These descriptions are contained in CCITT Recommendations I.321 [52] and I.413 [59]. In Figure 5.5 the lower layers of the B-ISDN PRM and their functions are illustrated. For the implementation of these functions, different fields within the cell header are used. These fields will be described in Section 5.4.2.

5.1.5.1   Cell Terminology

Before the functions of the individual layers of B-ISDN can be specified it is necessary to clarify the notion *cell* because it is used for definitions in the ATM layer as well as the physical layer.

The term *cell* is essential for B-ISDN, and therefore it is defined in CCITT Recommendation I.113 [45]:

> *A cell is a block of fixed length. It is identified by a label at the ATM layer of the B-ISDN PRM.*

More detailed definitions for the different kinds of cells are presented in CCITT Recommendation I.321 [52]:

> *Idle cell* (physical layer): A cell which is inserted/extracted by the physical layer in order to adapt the cell flow rate at the boundary between the ATM layer and the physical layer to the available payload capacity of the transmission system used.

> *Valid cell* (physical layer): A cell whose header has no errors or has been modified by the cell header error control (HEC) verification process (for HEC see Section 5.3.1.5).

> *Invalid cell* (physical layer): A cell whose header has errors and has not been modified by the cell HEC verification process. This cell is discarded at the physical layer.

> *Assigned cell* (ATM layer): A cell which provides a service to an application using the ATM layer service.

> *Unassigned cell* (ATM layer): An ATM layer cell which is not an assigned cell.

Only assigned and unassigned cells are passed to the ATM layer from the physical layer. The other cells carry no information concerning the ATM and higher layers and therefore they will only be processed by the physical layer.

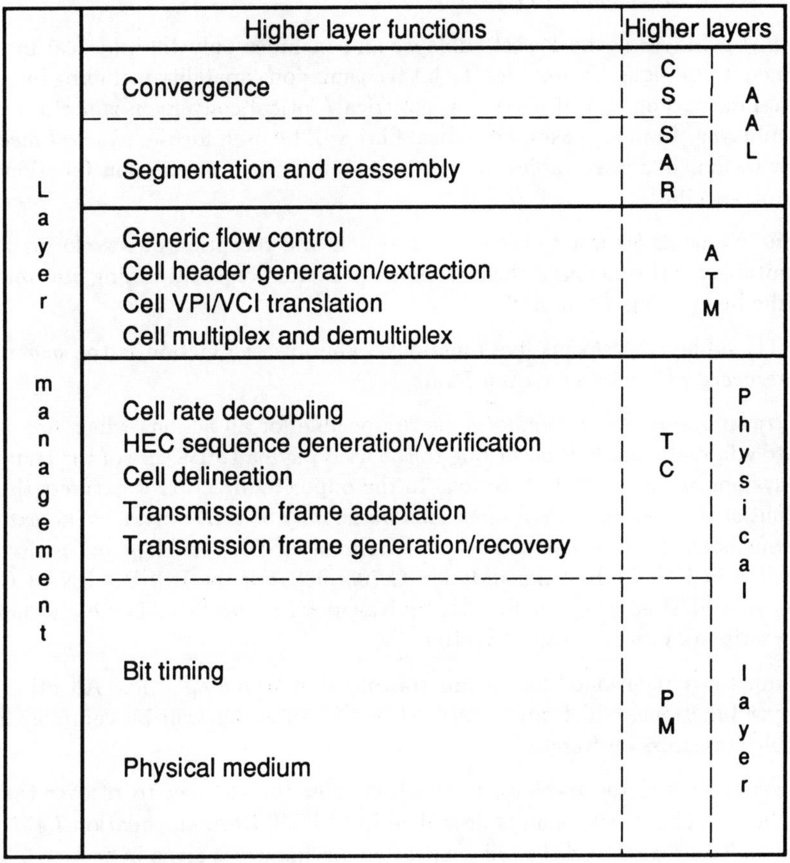

	Higher layer functions	Higher layers	
L a y e r **m a n a g e m e n t**	Convergence	C S	A A L
	Segmentation and reassembly	S A R	
	Generic flow control Cell header generation/extraction Cell VPI/VCI translation Cell multiplex and demultiplex	A T M	
	Cell rate decoupling HEC sequence generation/verification Cell delineation Transmission frame adaptation Transmission frame generation/recovery	T C	P h y s i c a l
	Bit timing Physical medium	P M	l a y e r

AAL	ATM adaptation layer	SAR	Segmentation and reassembly
ATM	Asynchronous transfer mode	TC	Transmission convergence
CS	Convergence sublayer	VCI	Virtual channel identifier
HEC	Header error control	VPI	Virtual path identifier
PM	Physical medium		

Figure 5.5: *The functions of B-ISDN in relation to the B-ISDN PRM*

5.1.5.2   Physical Layer Functions

The physical layer is subdivided into the *physical medium* (PM) sublayer and the *transmission convergence* (TC) sublayer.

The PM sublayer is the lowest sublayer and includes only the physical medium dependent functions. It provides the bit transmission capability including bit alignment. Line coding and, if necessary, electrical/optical conversion is performed by this sublayer. In many cases, an optical fibre will be used for the *physical medium*. Other media, like coax cables, are also possible. The transmission functions are medium specific.

The functions of *bit timing* are the generation and reception of waveforms which are suitable for the medium, the insertion and extraction of bit timing information, and the line coding if required.

The TC sublayer performs five functions. The lowest function is the *generation and recovery of the transmission frame*.

The *transmission frame adaptation* is responsible for all actions which are necessary to adapt the cell flow according to the used payload structure of the transmission system in the sending direction. In the opposite direction it extracts the cell flow out of the transmission frame. This frame may be cell equivalent (no external envelope is used), a *synchronous digital hierarchy* (SDH) envelope or an envelope according to CCITT Recommendation G.703 [33]. For the B-ISDN UNI, CCITT proposes a SDH envelope or the cell equivalent structure [62]. These alternatives are described in more detail in Section 5.3.

The functions mentioned so far are transmission frame specific. All other TC sublayer functions, which are presented in the following, can be common to all possible transmission frames.

Cell delineation is the mechanism which enables the receiver to recover the cell boundaries. This mechanism is described in CCITT Recommendation I.432 [62]. The detailed procedure of the cell delineation mechanism is given in Section 5.3.1.6. To protect the cell delineation mechanism from malicious attack the information field of a cell will be scrambled before transmission. Descrambling will be done at the receiving side.

HEC sequence generation is done in the transmit direction. The HEC sequence is inserted in its appropriate field within the header. At the receiving side the HEC value is recalculated and compared with the received value. If possible, header errors are corrected, otherwise the cell will be discarded. The details of the HEC mechanism are presented in Section 5.3.1.5.

In the sending direction the *cell rate decoupling* mechanism inserts idle cells in order to adapt the rate of ATM cells to the payload capacity of the transmission system. In the receiving direction this mechanism suppresses all idle cells. Only assigned and unassigned cells are passed to the ATM layer.

5.1.5.3 ATM Layer Functions

The layer above the physical layer is the ATM layer. Its characteristic features are independent of the physical medium. Four functions of this layer have been identified.

In the transmit direction, cells from individual VPs and VCs are multiplexed into one resulting cell stream by the *cell multiplexing* function. The composite stream is normally a non-continuous cell flow. At the receiving side the *cell demultiplexing* function splits the arriving cell stream into the individual cell flows appropriate to the VP or VC.

At ATM switching nodes and/or at cross-connect nodes, the *VPI and VCI translation* has to be performed. Within a VP switch the value of the VPI field of each incoming cell is translated into a new VPI value for the outgoing cell. At a VC switch the values of the VPI as well as the VCI are translated into new values.

The *cell header generation/extraction* function is applied at the termination points of the ATM layer. In the transmit direction, after receiving the cell information field from the AAL, the cell header generation adds the appropriate ATM cell header except for the HEC value. VPI/VCI values could be obtained by a translation from the SAP identifier. In the opposite direction the cell header extraction function removes the cell header. Only the cell information field is passed to the AAL. This function could also translate a VPI/VCI into a SAP identifier.

The *GFC* function is only defined at the B-ISDN UNI. GFC supports the control of the ATM traffic flow in a customer network. It can be used to alleviate short-term overload conditions (more details can be found in Section 5.4.2.2). The specific GFC information is carried in assigned or unassigned cells.

5.1.5.4 ATM Adaptation Layer Functions

The AAL is subdivided into the *segmentation and reassembly* (SAR) sublayer and the *convergence sublayer* (CS). The functions of the AAL are described in CCITT Recommendation I.362 [55].

The AAL is between the ATM layer and higher layers. Its basic function is the enhanced adaptation of the services provided by the ATM layer to the requirements of the higher layer. Higher layer PDUs are mapped into the information field of an ATM cell. The AAL entities exchange information with their peer AAL entities to support the AAL functions.

The functions of the AAL are organized in two sublayers. The essential functions of the SAR sublayer are, at the transmitting side, the segmentation of higher layer PDUs into a suitable size for the information field of the ATM cell (48 octets) and, at the receiving side, the reassembly of the particular information fields into higher layer PDUs. The CS is service dependent and provides the AAL service at the AAL-SAP.

Between these two sublayers, no SAP has yet been defined. The need for such SAPs needs further study. Different SAPs for higher layers can be achieved by different combinations of SAR and CS. For some applications, neither a CS nor a SAR is necessary and therefore they will be empty.

To minimize the number of AAL protocols, CCITT proposed a service classification which is specific to the AAL. This classification was made with respect to the following parameters:

- Timing relation

- Bit rate

- Connection mode.

Figure 5.6 depicts the foreseen AAL classes. Not all possible combinations make sense and therefore only four classes are distinguished.

	Class A	Class B	Class C	Class D
Timing relation between source and destination	Required		Not required	
Bit rate	Constant	Variable		
Connection mode	Connection oriented			Connection-less

Figure 5.6: *Service classification for AAL*

Some examples for the different service classes are listed below:

Class A:	Circuit emulation (e.g. transport of a 2 Mbit/s or 45 Mbit/s signal), constant bit rate video
Class B:	Variable bit rate video and audio
Class C:	Connection-oriented data transfer
Class D:	Connectionless data transfer

5.1.6   Primitives and Information Flows

5.1.6.1   Physical Layer and ATM Layer Primitives

Until now, in CCITT Recommendation I.321 [52], only physical layer and ATM layer primitives are defined. For the physical layer these are the following two types:

1. PH-DATA-REQUEST: The ATM layer requests the physical layer that the SDU associated with this primitive should be transported to its peer.

2. PH-DATA-INDICATION: The ATM layer is notified by the physical layer that the SDU associated with this primitive coming from its peer is available.

In certain applications (e.g. traffic shaping or GFC) the ATM layer may need information about each idle cell which has been discarded by the physical layer. The definition of primitives for this purpose is under study.

Between the ATM layer and the AAL, two primitives are also used:

1. ATM-DATA-REQUEST: The AAL requests the ATM layer that the ATM-SDU associated with this primitive should be transported to its peer.

2. ATM-DATA-INDICATION: The AAL is notified by the ATM layer that the ATM-SDU associated with the primitive coming from its peer is available.

The definition of other ATM layer primitives needs further study.

5.1.6.2   Information Flows of the Physical Layer

In the following section the information flows concerning the physical layer according to CCITT Recommendation I.413 [59] are presented. Different information flows exist:

- between the physical layer and the ATM layer
- between the physical layer and the management plane
- inside the physical layer between the sublayers.

From the PM sublayer to the TC sublayer, a flow of logical symbols (e.g. bits) and its associated timing information is exchanged. This information is also transferred in the opposite direction.

The information crossing the boundary between the physical layer and the ATM layer is always associated with one of the two primitives mentioned in Section 5.1.6.1. The physical layer provides the ATM layer with all cells belonging to this layer, with timing information and a clock derived from the line rate of the physical layer. In the opposite direction, assigned and unassigned cells, if any are available, and their associated timing are delivered.

The physical layer informs the management plane about the loss of the incoming signal and the indication of received errors or degraded error performance. Bit errors may be detected by unexpected code violations or other mechanisms. The information transfer in the opposite direction needs further study.

5.1.7 Relationship of OAM Functions with the B-ISDN PRM

The relationship between OAM functions and the B-ISDN PRM is presented in CCITT Recommendation I.610 [64]. For the OAM functions which are allocated to the layer management, a layered approach is used. The different functions of the layer management are correlated with various layers. The independence requirement and the layered concept lead to the following principles:

1. OAM functions related to OAM levels are independent of the OAM capabilities of other layers and have to be introduced at each layer.

2. Each layer has its own OAM processing to obtain quality and status information. The obtained results are delivered to the layer management or, if required, to the adjacent higher layer.

5.2 General Aspects of the User-Network Interface

5.2.1 Transfer Mode

As was mentioned in Chapter 1, the B-ISDN user-network interface (UNI) fully exploits the flexibility inherent in ATM. This means that the payload capacity of the interface (i.e. the whole of the transmission capacity besides the small portion that is needed to operate the interface properly, cf. Section 5.3.1) is completely structured into ATM cells.

As at the UNI, there is no pre-assignment of cells to specific user applications; the actual use of cells for connections to be established across the interface can change dynamically. Different traffic mixes can easily be supported as long as the cell transfer capacity is not exceeded. (How this is related to the interface bit rate will be discussed later.)

5.2.2 Bit Rates

As already mentioned in Section 3.3, two different interface bit rates are foreseen: one around 150 Mbit/s and the other around 600 Mbit/s. The exact figures will be discussed in a moment.

The 150 Mbit/s interface is symmetric with respect to bit rate, i.e. it offers 150 Mbit/s in the network-to-user direction and in the user-to-network direction as well. This sort of interface will predominantly be used for interactive services like telephony, video-telephony and data services. The extension of such an interface to a higher bit rate in order to be able to meet the needs of users with large traffic volumes seems quite natural. Thus, a bit rate symmetric 600 Mbit/s interface was also conceived. (The reason for choosing 600 Mbit/s will soon become clearer.) Users who are expected to have a much higher traffic load from the network to themselves than in the other direction may get an asymmetric version of the 600 Mbit/s interface with a reduced upstream capacity (user-to-network direction) of only 150 Mbit/s. The latter interface type would, for example, be suitable for simultaneous transmission of several television programmes to a residential customer who only needs the standard capacity for interactive services but a higher bit rate for distribution services like TV or sound programmes.

The definition of two separate interface bit rates was a compromise between two diverging requirements, namely a very limited number of different interface types on the one side and the cost-effectiveness of the interface on the other side.

The exact interface bit rates are:

- 155.520 Mbit/s
- 622.080 Mbit/s.

These bit rates are identical to the two lowest bit rates of the SDH as defined in CCITT Recommendation G.707 [34]. SDH is a new transmission hierarchy which was adopted by CCITT in 1988 [34, 35, 36]. It is based on the North-American SONET concept [6] that was developed with the main goal to:

- set a standard for optical transmission in order to react on the upcoming variety of manufacturer-specific implementations of optical transmission systems and interfaces

- provide transmission facilities with flexible add/drop capabilities to allow for simpler multiplexing/demultiplexing of signals than in the existing plesiochronous digital hierarchy (PDH) [32]

- grant generously dimensioned transmission overhead capacity to cater for various existing and assumed network operation and maintenance applications that were not, or at least only with difficulties, realizable in PDH.

More details on SDH can be found in Sections 5.3.1.1, 5.3.1.2 and 5.7, Chapter 7 as well as in [20].

5.2.3 Interface Structure

SDH has an inherent flexibility to transport quite different types of signals like ISDN channels, according to CCITT Recommendation I.412 [58], or ATM cells.

So SDH – being a universal transmission concept – was proposed as the B-ISDN interface structure [24]. Such a user-network interface implementation would have the advantage of full compatibility of the user-network interface with the network-node interface. This avoids otherwise necessary conversion of signals that are sent from the user through the network to other users. This property is extremely useful in the introductory phase of B-ISDN where a complete network infrastructure does not yet exist. Customers may easily be provided with access to a broadband network node which is a cross-connect or a switch and which may be located in a place different to that of the 64 kbit/s ISDN local exchange that usually serves the customer, via SDH equipment, which in some networks will be implemented prior to the realization of B-ISDN.

However, the SDH-based B-ISDN user-network interface has some drawbacks. A minor one is the fact that the large overhead capacity provided by SDH is not actually needed at the user-network interface, but some Mbit/s in relation to a 150 Mbit/s interface bit rate; however, this is no stringent argument against using SDH. Generation of the byte-structured SDH frame (cf. Figure 5.7) requires additional interface functionality that would not be necessary if the interface was completely cell structured (this is a possible solution as no 'physical' channels are foreseen, as in the case of the 64 kbit/s ISDN – cf. CCITT Recommendation I.412 [58]). Insertion of ATM cells from several terminals into one SDH frame in a passive bus configuration (such a configuration was standardized for the 64 kbit/s ISDN, see CCITT Recommendation I.430 [60]) is almost impossible for realistic transmission lengths due to individually varying transmission delays and the high bit rates involved. (Though passive configurations are no longer foreseen in CCITT Recommendation I.413 [59] this was put forward as an argument in favour of the cell-based interfaces.)

For these reasons, two interface types were standardized [59, 62]: one based on SDH and the other based on mere cell multiplexing (see Figure 5.7).

Whereas the SDH interface is ready to be implemented, the cell-based interface is not yet fully defined, e.g. coding and allocation of OAM functions is not sufficiently clear (cf. Sections 5.3.1 and 5.7). Remarkably, though the interface bit rate of the cell-based interface is basically not determined by any frame structure but might freely be chosen, it was agreed within CCITT to adopt the same bit rate (and payload capacity, see Section 5.3.1) for both interface types in order to facilitate interworking between the cell-based UNI and SDH in the network.

5.2.4   B-ISDN UNI Reference Configuration and Physical Realizations

As already mentioned in Section 4.7.1 the ISDN reference configuration for the basic access and primary rate access [57] was applied to B-ISDN with only minor modifications of notation. A reference configuration of the user-network access is

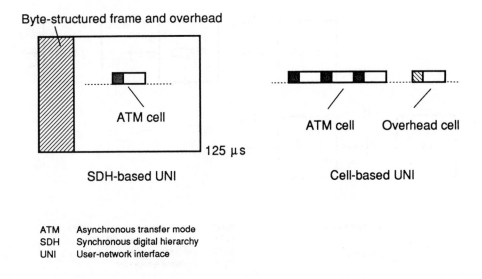

Byte-structured frame and overhead

ATM cell

125 µs

SDH-based UNI

ATM cell   Overhead cell

Cell-based UNI

ATM   Asynchronous transfer mode
SDH   Synchronous digital hierarchy
UNI   User-network interface

Figure 5.7: *User-network interface options*

a generic description based on the following two elements:

- Functional groups
- Reference points

as shown in Figure 5.8.

Figure 5.8 mainly shows broadband functional groups and reference points. The corresponding entities for the 64 kbit/s ISDN are described in CCITT Recommendation I.411 [57].

The broadband network termination B-NT1 includes functions broadly equivalent to layer 1 of the OSI reference model [80]. Examples of B-NT1 functions are (according to CCITT Recommendation I.413 [59]):

- Line transmission termination
- Transmission interface handling
- OAM functions.

The network termination B-NT2 includes functions broadly equivalent to layer 1 and higher layers of the OSI reference model. Examples of B-NT2 functions are [59]:

- Adaptation functions for different interface media and topologies

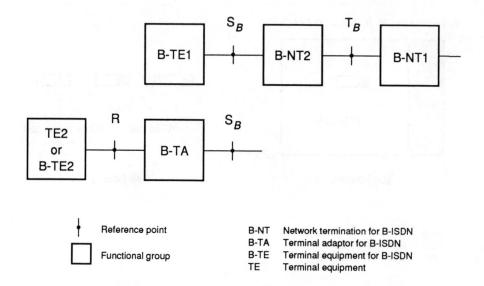

Figure 5.8: *B-ISDN UNI reference configuration*

- Multiplexing/demultiplexing/concentration of traffic

- Buffering of ATM cells

- Resource allocation; usage parameter control

- Signalling protocol handling

- Interface handling

- Switching of internal connections.

The generic term 'B-NT2' covers a host of actual implementations: it may be non-existent ('null B-NT2' provided that the interface definitions allow direct connection of terminals to the B-NT1), consist solely of layer 1 connections (wires), provide concentrating and/or multiplexing functions, or be a full-blown switch (private branch exchange). The B-NT2 functions may be concentrated or distributed, e.g. in a bus or ring with its access nodes (cf. Section 4.7).

S_B and T_B denote reference points between the terminal and the B-NT2, and the B-NT1 and B-NT2, respectively. Physical interfaces need not occur at a reference point in any case, e.g. B-NT1 and B-NT2 functions might be combined as shown in Figure 5.9.

It is also possible for the terminal to include B-NT2 functionality (see Figure 5.10).

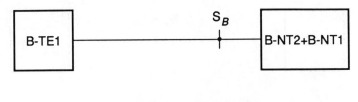

B-NT   Network termination for B-ISDN
B-TE   Terminal equipment for B-ISDN

Figure 5.9: *Configuration with physical interface at S_B only*

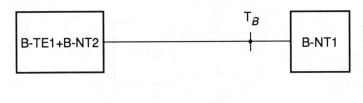

B-NT   Network termination for B-ISDN
B-TE   Terminal equipment for B-ISDN

Figure 5.10: *Configuration with physical interface at T_B only*

If the same interface standard applies to both S_B and T_B, S_B and T_B may coincide (see Figure 5.11), thus permitting direct connection of a terminal to the B-NT1.

B-ISDN will also offer 64 kbit/s ISDN services and interfaces. Terminals TE1 complying with CCITT Recommendation I.430 [60] (basic access) can be connected via such standard interfaces at the S reference point (as depicted in Figure 5.12).

Of course the B-NT2 may provide multiple interfaces of each type at S and S_B reference points.

Finally, to complete this brief description of the B-ISDN reference configurations, let us address the lower part of Figure 5.8 showing the functional groups B-TA (broadband terminal adaptor) and TE2/B-TE2, and the R reference point between both functional groups. Whereas at S_B and T_B standardized broadband interfaces (according to CCITT Recommendation I.432 [62]; see Section 5.3) must occur, at R any other (non-ISDN) interface is used to connect a non-ISDN terminal (indicated as TE2 or B-TE2 in the figure denoting a narrowband terminal or broadband terminal, respectively).

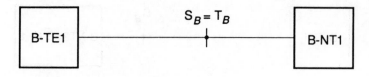

B-NT   Network termination for B-ISDN
B-TE   Terminal equipment for B-ISDN

Figure 5.11: *Coinciding S_B and T_B*

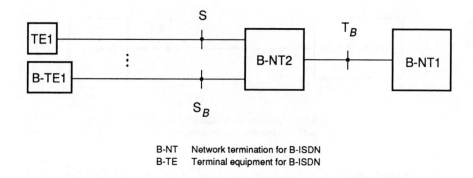

B-NT   Network termination for B-ISDN
B-TE   Terminal equipment for B-ISDN

Figure 5.12: *B-NT2 offering 64 kbit/s interfaces and broadband interfaces*

The provision of multiple terminal interfaces by the B-NT2 as indicated in Figure 5.12 is not restricted to a specific topology; star, bus, ring configurations or even mixtures of those topologies, e.g. starred bus, are possible (see Figure 5.13).

It may have become obvious from the foregoing figures that the B-ISDN standard allows many types of implementations according to the customers' needs. However, CCITT Recommendation I.413 [59] contains two restrictions:

1. At T_B reference point, only one interface per B-NT1 is allowed.

2. The interfaces are point-to-point at the physical layer 'in the sense that there is only one sink (receiver) in front of one source (transmitter)' [59]. (This means that passive bus configurations are not supported. As such configurations are strongly restricted in terms of the number of connectable terminals and coverable transmission distance, they have been excluded as not appropriate for broadband.)

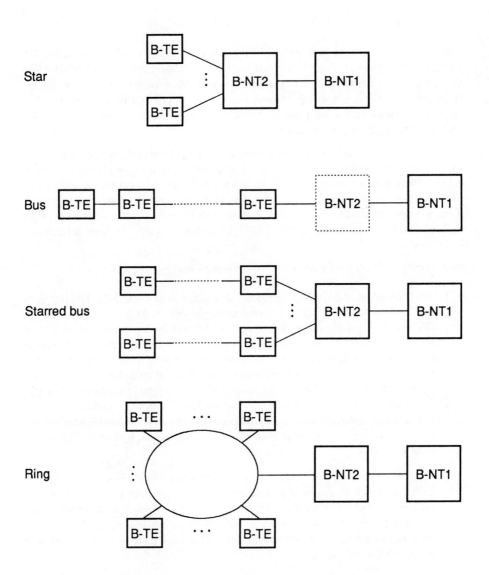

B-NT   Network termination for B-ISDN
B-TE   Terminal equipment for B-ISDN
Dashed box means the B-NT2 may or may not exist

Figure 5.13: *Multiple interface arrangements*

5.2.5   Special Issues

Configurations like that in Figure 5.11 require a high degree of commonality between the interfaces at S_B and T_B reference points. Of course the terminal interface at S_B should be unique in order to support worldwide terminal interchangeability. However, whether the last requirement can be met is not certain as currently two interface options at T_B exist (see Section 5.2.3) and there is strong support for interfaces being identical at S_B and T_B.

Another important issue is how, and to what extent, the standard interface should support shared medium configurations (bus/ring structures as shown in Figure 5.13). Such configurations require medium access control functions which can either be part of the standard interface functionality, or otherwise have to be implemented whenever necessary in additional medium access control entities. (This problem, which impacts the B-ISDN UNI definition, has already been introduced in Section 4.7.4.)

In a shared medium configuration, two different operation modes exist:

1. *Distributed multiplexing distributed demultiplexing (DMDD)*: DMDD is a mechanism for collecting cells from multiple terminals for service at the B-NT2 or the local exchange. In the opposite direction it provides a mechanism for distribution of cells to multiple terminals. In the downstream direction (network towards terminal) a terminal copies cells pertaining to it. In the upstream direction (opposite direction) the terminal waits for an idle or unassigned cell which can be used to transport information towards the network. Such a terminal is called *unidirectional* because it can only send its own cells towards the network and receive cells pertaining to it from the network direction. All cells for internal communication are served by the B-NT2 or the local exchange.

2. *LAN-like switching (LLS)*: In this operation mode, *bidirectional* terminals are used. A terminal can receive and send cells in both directions. Therefore, cells used for internal communication can be served locally without involving the B-NT2 or the local exchange. This mode unburdens the B-NT2 or the local exchange from switching functions. But LLS increases the complexity within the terminal.

In a star configuration as well as in a dual bus configuration using DMDD, only unidirectional terminals are necessary. The same type of terminal can be used as an *end-terminal* in the dual bus system operating in the LLS mode. All other terminals in a dual bus with LLS are bidirectional. This is not in contradiction to the requirement of terminal interchangeability: bidirectional terminals are able to operate in the unidirectional mode, too. So the customer has the choice between the fully interchangeable bidirectional terminal and the simpler unidirectional one whose applicability is somewhat restricted but may suffice in certain cases.

5.3 Physical Layer of the User-Network Interface

According to the B-ISDN protocol reference model already described in Section 5.1 the physical layer is split into two sublayers. These sublayers and the functions they provide are repeated in Figure 5.14.

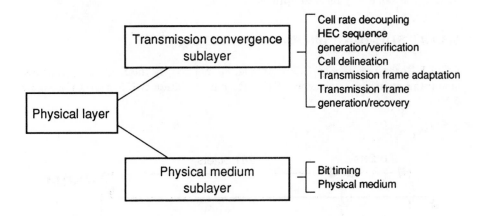

HEC   Header error control

Figure 5.14: *Physical layer structure*

The sublayer functions shown in Figure 5.14 have already been defined in Section 5.1. In the following their detailed description based on CCITT Recommendation I.432 [62] will be given. Operation and maintenance aspects are treated in Section 5.7.

5.3.1 Functions of the Transmission Convergence Sublayer

At the physical bit level the B-ISDN user-network interface has a bit rate of 155.520 Mbit/s or 622.080 Mbit/s, respectively. The *interface transfer capability* is defined as [62]:

> ... *the bit rate available for user information cells, signalling cells and ATM and higher layer OAM information cells, excluding physical layer related OAM information, transported in bytes or cells.*

Its value is 149.760 Mbit/s for the 155.520 Mbit/s interface and complies with SDH. The transfer capability of the 622.080 Mbit/s interface is about four times 149.760 Mbit/s.

In the following the transmission frame generation/adaptation aspects of the two interface options (SDH-based and cell-based) are described separately as they are rather different.

The other transmission convergence sublayer functions can in principle be performed the same way in both options.

5.3.1.1   SDH-Based Interface at 155.520 Mbit/s

CCITT Recommendations G.707-709 [34, 35, 36] specify the SDH. The transmission frame structure as given in CCITT Recommendation G.709 is shown in Figure 5.15.

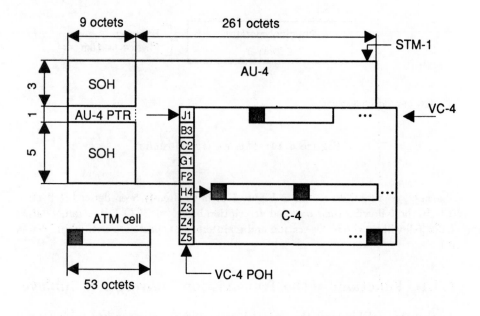

ATM	Asynchronous transfer mode	PTR Pointer
AU	Administrative unit	SOH Section overhead
C	Container	STM-1 Synchronous transport module 1
POH	Path overhead	VC-4 Virtual container 4

Figure 5.15: *Frame structure of the 155.520 Mbit/s SDH-based interface*

This frame is byte-structured and consists of 9 rows and 270 columns. The frame repetition frequency is 8 kHz (9×270 byte $\times$ 8 kHz = 155.520 Mbit/s). The first 9 columns comprise the section overhead (SOH) and the AU-4 pointer. Another 9 byte column is dedicated to the path overhead (POH).

This structuring of transmission overheads complies with the OAM levels introduced in Section 4.6.2. The use of these overhead bytes will be described in Section 5.7.

The generation of the SDH-based user-network interface signal is as follows [62]: first the ATM cell stream is mapped into the C-4 (the SDH terminology is defined in CCITT Recommendation G.708 [35]; here it is sufficient to say that C-4 is a 9 row $\times$ 260 column container corresponding to the transfer capability of 149.760 Mbit/s), then C-4 is packed in the virtual container VC-4 along with the VC-4 POH. The ATM cell boundaries are aligned with the byte boundaries of the frame. Note that an ATM cell may cross a C-4 boundary; as the C-4 capacity (2340 bytes) is not an integer multiple of the cell length (53 bytes) and the C-4 capacity is entirely used for cell mapping, this will indeed normally happen.

The virtual container VC-4 is then mapped into the 9×270 byte frame (which is called STM-1).

In principle, the first VC-4 byte can be located elsewhere in the STM-1 frame (excluding the first 9 SOH columns). The AU-4 pointer of the STM-1 frame is used to find the first VC-4 byte. The POH bytes J1, B3, C2, G1 and H4 are activated (for the meaning of these bytes, see Section 5.7). The H4 pointer will be set at the sending side to indicate the next occurrence of a cell boundary. This cell boundary indication may optionally be used at the receiving side to supplement the mandatory HEC-based cell delineation mechanism (cf. Section 5.3.1.5).

Permitted H4 values range from 0 to 52; this value indicates the offset in bytes from the H4 position to the first cell boundary following the H4 byte in the C-4 payload. The bit allocation for the H4 byte is given in Figure 5.16.

Unused	Unused	Cell offset indicator					
		MSB					LSB
1	2	3	4	5	6	7	8

LSB Least significant bit
MSB Most significant bit

Figure 5.16: *H4 bit allocation for ATM cell mapping into STM-1*

5.3.1.2 SDH-Based Interface at 622.080 Mbit/s

There is a straightforward way of creating a 622.080 Mbit/s frame (STM-4) from four STM-1s according to CCITT Recommendation G.708 (see Figure 5.17).

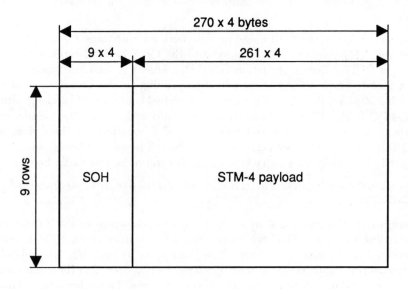

SOH   Section overhead
STM-4 Synchronous transport module 4

Figure 5.17: *STM-4 structure*

However, the STM-4 payload can be structured in several ways, e.g. simply as 4 × VC-4 or as one block. The available ATM cell transfer capability would be 4 × 149.760 Mbit/s = 599.040 Mbit/s in the first case and could be slightly more in the latter, as one payload block may need only one POH column (the exact figure for this case is [9 × 261 × 4 bytes - 9 bytes POH] × 8 kHz = 600.768 Mbit/s).

An asset of the second option that is much more important than the possible gain of an extra ATM cell transfer capability of 1.728 Mbit/s is the unrestricted use of about 600 Mbit/s for ATM cell mapping. Possible future applications requiring more than the VC-4 capacity can easily be allocated bandwidth elsewhere in the 600 Mbit/s payload block. Therefore, CCITT agreed on choosing this option (the payload may be restricted to 4 × 149.760 Mbit/s).

5.3.1.3   Cell-Based Interface

This interface consists of a continuous stream of cells (see Figure 5.18); each cell contains 53 octets.

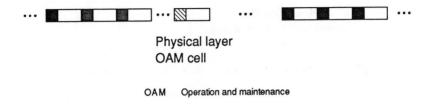

Physical layer
OAM cell

OAM   Operation and maintenance

Figure 5.18: *Cell-based interface structure*

Physical layer OAM information (which in the SDH case is allocated to SOH and POH) is here conveyed in specific physical layer OAM cells which are identified by unique cell header bit patterns that are reserved exclusively for these cell types. (This means that the ATM layer must not use these bit combinations as code points for the corresponding cell header fields, which are shown in Figure 5.26 on page 85.) The patterns are presented in Figure 5.19.

PL OAM cell type	Octet 1	Octet 2	Octet 3	Octet 4	Octet 5
F1				00000011	HEC
F2	00000000	00000000	00000000	00000101	valid
F3				00001001	code

HEC   Header error control
OAM   Operation and maintenance
PL   Physical layer

Figure 5.19: *Header pattern for physical layer OAM cells*

Physical layer OAM cells can be inserted in the cell stream in different ways. One is to generate a framed structure by regularly inserting an OAM cell after 26 cells (see Figure 5.20).

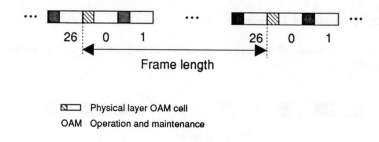

Physical layer OAM cell

OAM   Operation and maintenance

Figure 5.20: *Cell-based interface with frame structure*

This method automatically restricts the interface transfer capability to the requested value of 149.760 Mbit/s as the ratio 26:27 is the same as 149.760 Mbit/s to 155.520 Mbit/s.

The other method which is favoured by CCITT foresees *on-demand* insertion of physical layer OAM cells. The demand is to be determined by OAM requirements. (A maximum interval between two subsequent physical layer OAM cells of the same type F1, F2, F3 – if implemented – must not be exceeded.)

5.3.1.4   Cell Rate Decoupling

Whenever no assigned, unassigned or physical layer OAM cell is available for transmission an *idle cell* will be inserted to adapt the cell stream to the transmission bit rate. At the receiving side, such idle cells will be discarded. The insertion and discard of idle cells is called *cell rate decoupling*.

Idle cells are identified by a standardized pattern for the cell header which is shown in Figure 5.21.

Octet 1	Octet 2	Octet 3	Octet 4	Octet 5
00000000	00000000	00000000	00000001	HEC valid code

HEC   Header error control

Figure 5.21: *Header pattern for idle cell identification*

The idle cell pattern of Figure 5.21 is used throughout the ATM network to identify idle cells.

Each octet of the information field of an idle cell is filled with 01 10 10 10.

5.3.1.5   Header Error Control

According to the B-ISDN protocol reference model (see Section 5.1) the ATM cell header error control (HEC) is a physical layer function, therefore it is described in CCITT Recommendation I.432 [62] entitled 'B-ISDN user-network interface – physical layer specification'. It should be noted that the HEC method standardized for the user-network interface can universally be employed in the ATM network.

We first describe the HEC generation algorithm and then its capabilities.

Every ATM cell transmitter calculates the HEC value across the first four octets of the cell header and inserts the result in the fifth octet (HEC field) of the cell header. The HEC value is defined as 'the remainder of the division (modulo 2) by the generator polynomial $x^8 + x^2 + x + 1$ of the product x^8 multiplied by the content of the header excluding the HEC field' [62] (the transmitter device computing this remainder presets its register to all 0s before performing the division), to which the fixed pattern '01010101' will be added modulo 2.

This HEC code is capable of:

- correcting single-bit errors
- detecting certain multiple-bit errors

in the ATM cell header. Both capabilities will be used by the equipment receiving ATM cells according to the state-event diagram depicted in Figure 5.22.

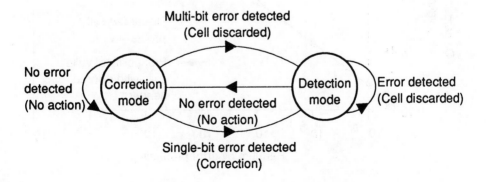

Figure 5.22: *HEC receiver actions*

After initialization the receiver is in 'correction mode'. When a single-bit error is detected, it will be corrected; when a multi-bit error is detected, the cell will be discarded. In both cases, transition into 'detection mode' takes place. In this receiver state, each cell with a detected error will be discarded; if no further errored cell is detected the receiver goes back to 'correction mode'.

The above mentioned receiver operation has been chosen to take into account the error characteristics of fibre-based transmission systems. These exhibit a mix of *single-bit errors* and relatively large *error bursts* (on a low error level). With the specified HEC method, recovery from single-bit errors is provided, and the probability of delivering cells with errored headers under bursty error conditions is kept low.

Figure 5.23 shows the HEC performance as a function of bit error probability.

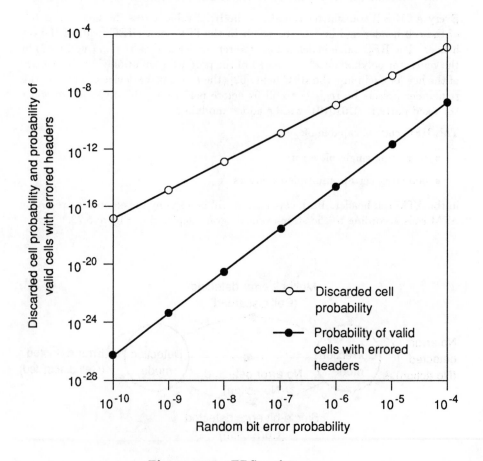

Figure 5.23: *HEC performance*

For a bit error probability of, say, 10^{-8} the probability for the discard of cells (due to header errors which have been recognized and could not be corrected) is about 10^{-13}, and the probability of valid cells with errored headers (these are cells with unrecognizable header errors) is about 10^{-20}.

5.3.1.6   Cell Delineation

'Cell delineation is the process which allows identification of the cell boundaries' [62].

The method recommended by CCITT [62] for cell delineation is based on the correlation between the header bits to be protected (the first four octets of the cell header) and the relevant control bits (one octet HEC field, cf. Section 5.3.1.5). Figure 5.24 shows the state diagram of the HEC-based cell delineation.

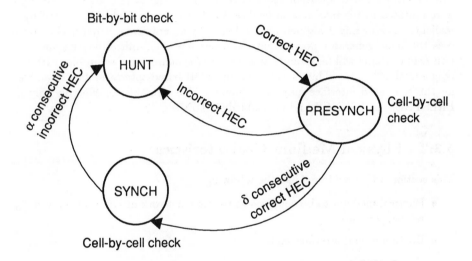

Figure 5.24: *Cell delineation state diagram*

In HUNT state, a bit-by-bit check of the assumed header field is performed. When more information is available (e.g. byte boundaries, or H4 pointer information in SDH, cf. Section 5.3.1.1), this may optionally be used. When the HEC coding law (see Section 5.3.1.5) is seen to be respected (i.e. syndrome equals zero), one assumes that a header has been found and goes to PRESYNCH state. Now the

HEC correlation check is performed cell by cell. If δ consecutive correct HECs are found, SYNCH state is entered; if not, the system goes back to HUNT state. SYNCH state is only left (to HUNT state) if α consecutive incorrect HECs are identified.

The values for α and δ obviously influence the performance of the cell delineation process. Robustness against false misalignment due to bit errors depends on α, while robustness against false delineation in the resynchronization phase depends on δ. The following values for α and δ have been suggested:

$$\alpha = 7, \quad \delta = 6$$

With $\alpha = 7$, a 155.520 Mbit/s ATM system will be in SYNCH for more than one year even when the bit error probability is about 10^{-4}. With $\delta = 6$, the same system with the same bit error probability will need about 10 cells or 28 μs to re-enter SYNCH after loss of cell synchronization [62].

The described cell delineation method could fail if the header HEC correlation were imitated in the information field of ATM cells. This might be effected by a malicious user or might happen inadvertently by an application that accidentally uses the same generator polynomial. To overcome such difficulties the information field contents will be scrambled using a self-synchronizing scrambler with the polynomial $x^{43} + 1$. (This is valid for the SDH-based interface; the scrambler for the cell-based interface may be different.) The scrambler is effective only in PRESYNCH and SYNCH and is disabled in HUNT.

5.3.2   Physical Medium Characteristics

This section addresses items like the following:

- Physical medium to be deployed at the user-network interface at S_B and T_B reference points
- Bit timing and interface code
- Power feeding
- Modes of operation of the interface (and necessary procedures).

5.3.2.1   Physical Medium

The future broadband integrated services broadband network will be based on the deployment of optical fibre transmission (cf. Section 3.3) in the trunk network and the user access network. However, it is not clear whether optical transmission should also be used at the interfaces at S_B and T_B reference points.

As the interface range at S_B and T_B is usually much shorter than the distances that have to be bridged in the access network, electrical media could alternatively be employed at S_B and T_B (at least for the 155.520 Mbit/s interface). Such an electrical interface was assessed to be cheaper (at least as a short- and medium-term solution) and easier to handle in terms of installation and maintenance. For the 155.520 Mbit/s interface, a range of up to about 200 m can be covered with an electrical interface; for the 622.080 Mbit/s interface the range of an electrical interface would considerably decrease to about 100 m [131].

Use of the same medium for 155.520 Mbit/s and 622.080 Mbit/s would support upgradability of the 155.520 Mbit/s interface to the higher bit rate. The same medium at S_B and T_B would allow for terminal portability from S_B to T_B. The optional use of both media at the interface at either reference point would require medium adaptors in all cases where equipment not complying with the actually implemented medium is to be used.

It should be noted that in the case of electrical interfaces longer interface ranges than 100 to 200 m can be achieved by, for example, insertion of an optical transmission system. This solution however requires electrical/optical conversion twice.

CCITT has specified both an electrical and an optical 155.520 Mbit/s interface to be applied at T_B. The electrical interface 'must cover a span from 0 to 100 m and possibly up to 200 m' [62] and shall consist of two coaxial cables, one for each direction. The wiring configuration is point to point. The parameters defined for the electrical 155.52 Mbit/s interface in CCITT Recommendation G.703 [33] 'should be used as appropriate' [62].

The optical interface 'must cover a span from 0 to 800 m and possibly up to 2 km' [62]. The optical medium (single-mode or multi-mode fibre, single or dual fibre etc.) and the optical parameters need further study. The optical parameters should be based on existing and upcoming optical standards (CCITT, ISO etc.).

CCITT Recommendation I.432 [62] has not yet specified the physical properties of the 155.520 Mbit/s interface at S_B reference point. Commonality between the interfaces at S_B and T_B is aimed at.

The feasibility and range of application of an electrical 622.080 Mbit/s interface needs further study. The parameters of an optical 622.080 Mbit/s interface should comply as much as possible with those of the optical 155.520 Mbit/s interface.

More information on the physical medium characteristics of the 155.520 Mbit/s interface is presented in Tables 5.2 and 5.3. The contents of these tables are so-called *study points* with possible solutions which have been proposed to CCITT and which are presently under investigation (cf. [25, 27]).

5.3.2.2 Bit Timing and Interface Code

In normal operation, *timing* for the transmitter is locked to the timing received across the interface. Timing may alternatively be provided locally by the clock of the customer equipment in the case of the cell-based interface option. Locally

Study Point	Possible Solution
Interface range	About 100 m for microcoax cables
	About 200 m for CATV type cables
Transmission medium	Two coaxial cables, one for each direction
Electrical parameters of input and output ports	Attenuation, pulse shape, test conditions etc. according to 155.520 Mbit/s interface specification of CCITT Recommendation G.703 [33]; e.g. attenuation should follow approximate $\sqrt{f}$ law with a maximum insertion loss of 12.7 dB at a frequency of 78 MHz

Table 5.2: *155.520 Mbit/s electrical interface characteristics*

provided timing will be used under fault conditions; then the interface works in free running clock mode. For this mode, a tolerance $\pm$ 20 ppm has been defined (for the 155.520 Mbit/s interface).

As interface code, *coded mark inversion* (CMI) as described in CCITT Recommendation G.703 [33] was proposed for the 155.520 Mbit/s interface [25].

CMI has several advantages (cf. [131]):

- Simple implementation (e.g. easy clock extraction).

- Zero DC and low frequency content.

- Guaranteed signal transitions: the number of transitions in the encoded data stream is independent of the applied data stream. Bit sequence independence required for the interface [59] is easily achieved (and malicious attack to prevent timing extraction is made impossible).

- No bit error multiplication.

- Ability to trace discrete bit errors through code violations.

However, CMI has the drawback of doubling the transmission rate of the CMI-coded signal (baud rate = 2 $\times$ bit rate). This is not critical in the case of the 155.520 Mbit/s interface but is clearly disadvantageous for the 622.080 Mbit/s interface.

Alternatively, the use of *non-return-to-zero* (NRZ) code (cf. [42]) was proposed for the optical interface. However, it was also mentioned that it was advantageous to achieve commonality of those interface properties that are not strictly medium-dependent, as is the case for line coding. Also, jitter requirements should be aligned for both interface options – electrical and optical – in order to allow common implementation of jitter reduction functions. (Jitter performance requirements should be derived from CCITT Recommendation G.958 [43] for the optical

Study Point	Possible Solution
Interface range	2000 m or more
Operating wavelength	1. Around 1310 nm
	2. Around 780 nm
Medium characteristics	1. Single-mode fibres [31]
	2. Multi-mode fibres [30]
Transmission medium	Two fibres, one for each direction
Attenuation range	1. 1310 nm: 0 ... 7 dB or 0 ... 12 dB
	2. 780 nm: 0 ... 11 dB
	(the values for both options shall include margin, splice losses, aging, deterioration, ...)
Maximum dispersion	1. 1310 nm: 6 ps/km $\star$ nm
	2. 780 nm: 100 ps/km $\star$ nm
Input and output port characteristics	Source: Laser diode
	Launched power: -8 ... -15 dBm
	Minimum extinction ratio: 8.2 dB
	Minimum receiver sensitivity:
	1. 1310 nm: -23 dBm
	2. 780 nm: -26 dBm
	Minimum receiver overload (= maximum acceptable value of the received average power for a bit error rate of 10^{-10}): -8 dBm
	Optical path power penalty: values not exceeding 1 dB shall be tolerated
Safety	It may be necessary to provide an automatic shutdown of the laser to protect a user against radiation out of open connectors or in case of cable break

Table 5.3: *155.520 Mbit/s optical interface characteristics*

interface and from CCITT Recommendation G.823 [40] for the electrical interface [25].)

5.3.2.3 Power Feeding

A power feeding mechanism quite similar to that used for the primary rate access [61] is proposed in [25]. This method will briefly be described in the following.

A separate pair of wires at the interface at T_B reference point is thought to be able to power the B-NT1 via this interface. The power sink can be fed:

- either by a source under the responsibility of the user when requested by the network provider

- or by a power supply unit, under the responsibility of the network provider, connected to the mains electric supply on the customer's premises.

When power is provided by the user, the source may be an integral part of the B-NT2 or B-TE, or it may be physically separated from B-NT2 or B-TE as an individual power supply unit.

The power available at the B-NT1 via the user-network interface (at T_B) shall be at least 15 W, and the feeding voltage shall be in the range of -20 V to -57 V relative to ground.

The power source must be protected against short circuits and overload. The power sink of the B-NT1 should not be damaged by an interchange of wires.

5.3.2.4   Modes of Operation

The B-ISDN user-network interface is normally in the 'fully active' state [59]. Other modes of operation are under discussion, e.g. an emergency mode in the case of power failure, or a deactivated mode in order to save power. If activation/deactivation is to be implemented it will become necessary to define:

- activation/deactivation signals
- activation/deactivation procedures.

Deactivation of the interface would be used to minimize power consumption during idle periods when no connections are established. The emergency mode is necessary to guarantee minimum communication possibilities in the case of power failure, e.g. at least one telephone set should work. (This mode requires battery back-up in the B-NT1 and/or B-NT2.)

As to economizing on power consumption due to the establishment of a deactivated interface state, some arguments can be found in [90]. Deactivation allows for:

- extension of the time of the battery-powered operation under power failure conditions (i.e. deactivation is especially important in the emergency state)
- reduction of the heat management problem.

These benefits could be increased if activation/deactivation of the interface were accompanied by activation/deactivation of the line. In this case the network operator would also get relief in terms of power consumption and heat management at the local exchange or remote switching/multiplexing/concentrating unit.

In [90] it is reported that in the deactivated state the power consumption of the network termination and line termination is about one-half of the corresponding value in normal (fully active) mode. The time to go from deactivated state back to active state is estimated to be about 10 - 50 ms. The same handshake principle as described in CCITT Recommendation I.430 [60] for the basic access could be used as a basis for the activation/deactivation procedure in B-ISDN.

It should be noted that the transition of the interface from deactivated state to active state is not only a physical layer task but also impacts on higher layers, e.g. the ATM layer where recovery procedures may be necessary.

5.4 ATM Layer

CCITT Recommendation I.150 [48] includes the functional characteristics of the ATM layer and its specification is given in CCITT Recommendation I.361 [54].

5.4.1 Cell Structure

The *cell* is the basic element of the ATM layer. As already mentioned in Section 5.1.5.1 the term 'cell' is also used at the physical layer. A cell consists of a 5 octet header and a 48 octet information field. Its structure is shown in Figure 5.25.

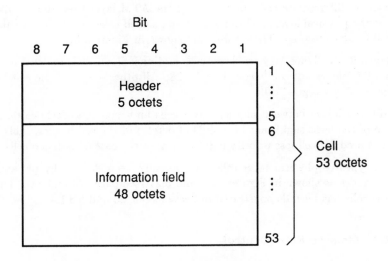

Figure 5.25: *Cell structure*

The following numbering conventions are defined in CCITT Recommendation I.361 [54]:

- Octets are sent in increasing order starting with octet 1. Therefore, the cell header will be sent first followed by the information field.

- Bits within an octet are sent in decreasing order starting with bit 8.

- For all fields, the first bit sent is the most significant bit (MSB).

5.4.2   Cell Header

The cell header at the B-ISDN user-network interface (UNI) differs from that at the B-ISDN network-node interface (NNI) in the use of bit 5 - 8 of octet 1. The B-ISDN NNI is the interface between network nodes (cf. Section 7.3). At the B-ISDN NNI these bits are part of the VPI, whereas at the B-ISDN UNI these bits constitute an independent unit, GFC. Figure 5.26 depicts the cell header used at the B-ISDN UNI and the B-ISDN NNI.

The different fields defined within the cell header have no meaning for physical layer cells. Their significance is restricted to ATM cells.

5.4.2.1   Pre-Assigned Cell Header Values

In order to differentiate cells for the use of the ATM layer from those cells only used at the physical layer, and to identify unassigned cells, pre-assigned values of the cell header are used. These values are shown in Figure 5.27.

As shown in the figure, physical layer cells and unassigned cells are characterized by an all-0 pattern of the header bits 5 - 28. All other values of the cell header can be used by assigned cells.

The differentiation between physical layer cells and unassigned cells is based on the use of the least significant bit (LSB) of octet 4 of the cell header. This bit is thus not used for cell loss priority indication as in the case of assigned cells.

Several types of physical layer cells have already been defined by pre-assigned header values as shown in Figures 5.19 and 5.21 (see pages 73 and 74). The use of these cells has been demonstrated in Sections 5.3.1.3 and 5.3.1.4.

5.4.2.2   Generic Flow Control

The *generic flow control* (GFC) field consists of 4 bits. Its default value is 0000 as long as the GFC function is not completely defined. But when the mechanism is standardized, all values of the GFC field will be available for coding. GFC information is carried either in *assigned* or *unassigned* cells [52].

The functional description of the GFC is included in CCITT Recommendation I.150 [48]. The GFC mechanism assists in the control of the traffic flow from

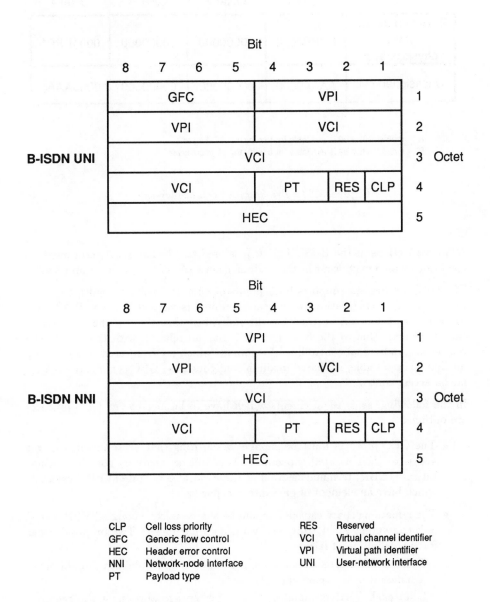

Figure 5.26: *Cell header at the B-ISDN UNI and the B-ISDN NNI*

	Octet 1	Octet 2	Octet 3	Octet 4
Reserved for use of the physical layer	PPPP0000	00000000	00000000	0000PPP1
Unassigned cell	AAAA0000	00000000	00000000	0000AAA0

A   indicates the bit is available for use by the ATM layer
P   indicates the bit is available for use by the physical layer

Figure 5.27: *Pre-assigned cell header values*

ATM connections at the B-ISDN UNI. It is used to alleviate short-term overload conditions which may occur in the customer network (cf. Sections 4.7 and 5.2.5).

The GFC mechanism supports both point-to-point and point-to-multipoint configurations. In configurations where each terminal is connected to the B-NT2 via its own line, GFC can be used for the individual throttling of the cell flow of each terminal. Due to the fact that GFC has no relation with the rest of the cell header, individual controlling of terminals which are connected to a common medium is impossible; in shared medium configurations, GFC is globally used for media access control.

In the following, some requirements which have to be met by the GFC protocol are outlined:

- The GFC protocol must be capable of ensuring that all terminals can get access to their assured capacities. This will be necessary for all constant bit rate (CBR) terminals as well as those variable bit rate (VBR) terminals which have an element of guaranteed capacity.

- The remaining spare capacity should be shared fairly among all VBR terminals contending for it. However, what does *fair* mean? Two proposals exist for the definition of fair:
  1. Each VBR terminal contending for additional bandwidth gets the same amount of the spare capacity.
  2. In each VBR terminal the same percentage portion of the required additional capacity should be satisfied.

- The GFC protocol should also support different delay and delay variation (jitter) requirements. For example, this can be fulfilled by introducing different priority levels.

- Direct terminal-to-terminal communication (without involving the B-NT2) in shared medium configurations should be possible. This requires a symmetrical implementation of the GFC procedure.

- The GFC protocol should be insensitive to the traffic mix (e.g. number of active CBR and VBR sources, bit rate mix) as well as the system parameters like number of terminals or distance between terminals.

- Sufficient robustness is required in the case of lost, errored or misinserted GFC information.

GFC is provided at the B-ISDN UNI, i.e. the GFC field is present at the interfaces at the S_B, T_B and SSB reference points. (Here the notation SSB – see Figure 5.28 – is used for shared medium configurations in order to distinguish between different locations of the terminal interface: S_B denotes the reference point between the B-NT2 and the first terminal, SSB the reference points between terminals.) GFC provides flow control for the information generated locally by terminals within the customer premises. This traffic may occur in directions to and from the terminal across the interfaces at S_B and SSB. GFC does not control the traffic flow originating from the network.

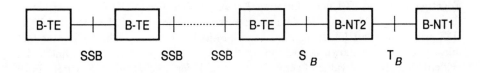

B-NT   Network termination for B-ISDN
B-TE   Terminal equipment for B-ISDN

Figure 5.28: *Scope of application of GFC*

An ATM network does not provide the sort of flow control which is implemented in packet networks and it has no facilities to store cells over a longer period of time. So inside an ATM network there is no need for GFC. GFC only controls terminals connected to a customer network.

The exact GFC procedure is not yet defined; however, several proposals have been made [101]. Some of the proposed GFC procedures are based on a distributed queueing algorithm which is well known from the DQDB network [108]. Modifications were necessary in order to support CBR traffic and to support different customer network topologies. Other proposals use a modified Orwell protocol [91] for controlling the cell flow of the terminals.

In order to find out the *best* protocol, values of some system and traffic parameters (e.g. number of active terminals, distances between terminals, service mix, bit rate mix) have been defined which will be the base for a performance evaluation. However, the decision cannot only be made on the obtained results. Other features like expense of implementation and reliability also have to be taken into account.

5.4.2.3   Virtual Path Identifier

The *virtual path identifier* (VPI) field at the B-ISDN UNI consists of 8 bits and is used for routing. The VPI at the NNI comprises the first 12 bits of the cell header, thus providing enhanced routing capabilities. For some special purposes, pre-assigned VPI values are used. As already mentioned in Section 5.4.2.1, all bits of the VPI field are set to zero in an unassigned cell. The same VPI value is chosen for the identification of the meta-signalling virtual channel and the general broadcast signalling virtual channel. Other uses of pre-assigned VPIs are not excluded.

5.4.2.4   Virtual Channel Identifier

Together with the VPI field the *virtual channel identifier* (VCI) field constitutes the routing field of a cell. A field of 16 bits is used for the VCI at the B-ISDN UNI as well as the NNI. It also has some pre-assigned values. The VCI value for unassigned cells is shown in Section 5.4.2.1. With this assignment in mind it is evident that the VCI value of zero is not available for user VC identification. Two other VCI values are also pre-assigned for special purposes:

Meta-signalling VCI: 00000000 00000001
General broadcast VCI: 00000000 00000010

Other pre-assigned VCI values may be defined in addition.

5.4.2.5   Payload Type

Two header bits are used for the *payload type* (PT) identification. Cells carrying user information are marked by PT 00. Other PT values for user information and for network information are not yet defined.

The payload of user information cells contains user information as well as service adaptation functions. In network information cells the payload is used to carry information the network needs for its operation and maintenance. One example is the F5 information flow (see Section 4.6.2) which supports OAM of VCCs. Here the PT identifier is used to distinguish between user cells and F5 cells pertaining to the same VCC.

Network information cells originate in the network but they may end beyond the B-ISDN UNI and may possibly be evaluated by the end user.

5.4.2.6   Reserved Field

Bit 2 of octet 4 of the cell header is the *reserved field*. The default value of this field is 0. Today its use is not specified. In the future the reserved field may be used for further enhancements of existing cell header functions or it may be used for up to now unknown header functions.

5.4.2.7   Cell Loss Priority

The *cell loss priority* (CLP) field consists of 1 bit and is used for explicit indication of the cell loss priority. If the value of the CLP bit is 1 the cell is subject to discard, depending on the network conditions. However, the agreed quality of service (QOS) parameters will not be violated. In the other case (CLP = 0) the cell has high priority and therefore sufficient network resources have to be allocated to it. The CLP bit may be set by the user or the service provider. Cells belonging to a CBR connection always have high priorities. Many VBR services require a guaranteed minimum capacity as well as a peak capacity. Some of these services may take advantage of the CLP bit to distinguish between cells of high and low loss sensitivity.

At the establishment of a VBR connection the rate of higher priority cells will be determined but it can be renegotiated during the connection phase. Cells of higher priority which exceed the agreed parameters are subject to the normal usage parameter control.

5.4.2.8   Header Error Control

This field is part of the cell header but it is not used by the ATM layer. It contains the *header error control* (HEC) sequence which is processed by the physical layer. The HEC mechanism is specified in CCITT Recommendation I.432 [62]. A description of the mechanism is given in Section 5.3.1.5.

5.4.3   ATM Layer Connections

An ATM layer connection is the concatenation of ATM layer links in order to provide an end-to-end transfer capability to access points.

The VPI is used to distinguish different VP links which are multiplexed at the ATM layer into the same physical layer connection at an interface in one direction. Inside a VPC the different VC links are identified by their individual VCIs.

Two VCs belonging to different VPs at the same interface may have identical VCI values. For a proper identification of a VC the VCI as well as the VPI are necessary.

A VPI is changed at points where a VP link is terminated (e.g. cross-connect, concentrator and switch). At points where VC links are terminated the VCI is changed. As a consequence, VCI values are preserved within a VPC.

5.4.3.1   Active Connections at the B-ISDN UNI

At the B-ISDN UNI, 24 bits are available for routing. However, the actual number of used bits is negotiated between the user and the network (e.g. on subscription basis). The lower requirements of the user or the network determine the number of active routing bits. The following rules are agreed by CCITT [54] for the determination of the position of active routing bits within the VPI/VCI field:

- The used bits of the VPI field as well as the VCI field will be contiguous.

- The bit allocation will always begin with the LSB of its appropriate field.

- Unallocated bits of the routing field, i.e. bits not used by the user or the network, will be set to zero.

5.4.3.2   Virtual Channel Connections

The *virtual channel connection* (VCC) is defined in CCITT Recommendation I.113 [45] as follows (cf. Section 4.2.1):

> *A concatenation of virtual channel links that extends between two points where the adaptation layer is accessed.*

For the establishment of a VCC at the B-ISDN UNI, one of four methods can be used:

1. Semi-permanent or permanent VCCs are established during the subscription time. No signalling procedure is necessary.

2. A VCC is established/released by using a meta-signalling procedure. This approach is applied for establishing a signalling VC (see Section 4.3.3).

3. Establishment/release of a switched end-to-end VCC can be done by a user-to-network signalling procedure.

4. If a VPC between two B-ISDN UNIs already exists, a VCC within this VPC can be established/released by employing a user-to-user signalling procedure.

The cell sequence integrity is preserved within a VCC. Traffic parameters are individually negotiated at VCC establishment between the user and the network.

These parameters can be renegotiated during the connection phase. All cells originating from the user are monitored by the network in order to ensure that the agreed parameters are not violated.

At VCC establishment the QOS for the connection is negotiated between the user and the network. The agreed QOS cannot be changed for the duration of the connection.

The VCI can be determined by the network or the user or by negotiation between network and user, or a standardized value will be used. In general the value of the VCI field is independent of the service provided over that VC. But for simplifying terminal interchangeability and initialization the same VCI value will be used at all B-ISDN UNIs for some fundamental functions (e.g. meta-signalling).

5.4.3.3   Virtual Path Connections

The definition of the *virtual path connection* (VPC) is given in CCITT Recommendation I.113 [45] (cf. Section 4.2.1):

> *A concatenation of virtual path links that extends between the point where the virtual channel identifier values are assigned and the point where those values are translated or removed.*

The methods for establishing/releasing a VPC between VPC endpoints are not yet defined but they may obey one of the following principles:

1. A VPC is established/released on a subscription basis and therefore no signalling procedure is necessary.

2. The VPC establishment/release may be controlled by the customer. For these purposes, signalling or network management procedures are utilized.

3. A VPC can also be established/released by the network using network signalling procedures.

Within a VPC the cell sequence integrity is preserved for each VCC carried. During VPC establishment the traffic parameters for the VPC are negotiated between the user and the network. If necessary, these parameters can subsequently be renegotiated. All input cells from the user to the network are monitored to supervise the agreed traffic parameters.

At VPC establishment the QOS is determined from a number of QOS classes supported by the network. The QOS class associated with a VPC cannot be changed during the duration of the VPC. A VPC can carry VCCs requiring different QOS classes. Therefore, the QOS of the VPC must meet the most demanding QOS of the VCCs carried.

Some VCIs within a VPC may not be available to the user, but may be reserved for, say, network OAM purposes (e.g. to implement the F4 flow, see Section 4.6.2).

5.5   ATM Adaptation Layer

The functions of the AAL have already been described in Section 5.1.5.4. The AAL provides the mapping of higher layer PDUs into the information field of cells and the reassembly of those PDUs. Other AAL functions support different applications. The detailed specification of the AAL (see also CCITT Recommendation I.363 [56]) is presented in the following.

Until now, four AAL protocol types are defined. Each type consists of a specific SAR sublayer and CS. This classification fits the AAL service classes described in Section 5.1.5.4 (e.g. CBR services of class A will use AAL type 1), however, no strict relationship between the AAL service classes and the AAL protocol types is requested. Other combinations of the described SAR and CS protocols or other SAR and/or CS protocols may also be used to support specific services. In some applications the SAR sublayer and/or CS may be empty, i.e. the AAL-PCI is not present, and the AAL functions are reduced to the reception/delivery of the ATM-SDUs.

5.5.1   AAL Type 1

5.5.1.1   Services and Functions

Normally, CBR services (class A) use AAL type 1 because it receives/delivers SDUs with constant bit rate from/to the layer above. It also transfers timing information between source and destination. Indication of lost or errored information is sent to the higher layer if these failures cannot be recovered within the AAL.

The functions which will be performed by the AAL are as follows:

- Segmentation and reassembly of user information

- Handling of cell delay variation

- Handling of lost and misinserted cells

- Source clock frequency recovery at the receiver

- Monitoring of AAL-PCI for bit errors as well as handling those errors

- Monitoring of the user information field for bit errors and possible corrective actions.

In the case of circuit emulation, monitoring of the end-to-end QOS is necessary, which will be located at the CS. For this purpose, a cyclic redundancy check (CRC) may be calculated for the information carried in one or more cells. The obtained result is transferred to the receiver within the information field of a cell or in a special OAM cell.

Circuit emulation is believed to be an important feature of B-ISDN as it allows for the transport of currently existing circuit-based signals (e.g. 1.5 Mbit/s or 2 Mbit/s), meeting the requirements on delay, jitter, bit error rate etc. for such signals. So the user will not even be aware of the transfer mechanism involved.

5.5.1.2 Segmentation and Reassembly Sublayer

The SAR-PDU consists of 48 octets. The first octet includes the PCI; all other octets are available for the payload. The PCI is subdivided into a 4 bit *sequence number* (SN) and a 4 bit *sequence number protection* (SNP). Figure 5.29 shows the SAR-PDU format for AAL type 1.

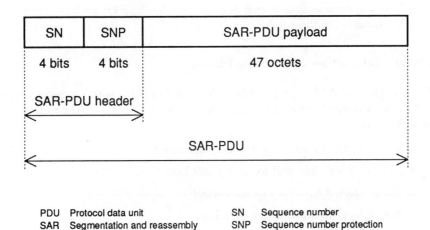

| PDU | Protocol data unit | SN | Sequence number |
| SAR | Segmentation and reassembly | SNP | Sequence number protection |

Figure 5.29: *Example of SAR-PDU format for AAL type 1*

The SN makes it possible to detect the loss or misinsertion of cells. A specific value of the SN can be used for a specific purpose, e.g. the existence of CS functions. The exact counting scheme is not yet defined.

The SNP provides error detection and correction capabilities. The following two step approach will be used which allows the correction of all 1 bit errors and the detection of all 2 bit errors:

1. The SN is protected by the polynomial $G(x) = x^3 + x + 1$.

2. The resulting 7 bit code word is protected by an even parity check.

5.5.1.3   Convergence Sublayer

The following functions may be performed by the CS:

- Some audio and video applications may require forward error correction to ensure high quality. This may be combined with bit interleaving to give more secure protection against errors.

- Clock recovery by monitoring the buffer filling, which may be necessary for some services, can also be performed by the CS. No specific field within the CS-PDU is required.

- Other services may demand an explicit time indication. This can be performed by a time stamp pattern inserted in the CS-PDU or by alternative methods.

- Loss and misinsertion of cells is recognized by the SAR protocol. However, the handling of these failures is done in the CS.

5.5.1.4   Interaction with Other Planes

The user plane of AAL type 1 will interchange information with the control plane and the management plane. The following information is transferred to the management plane:

- Errors in the transmission of user information
- Cells have been lost and unknown cells have been inserted
- The received AAL-PCI was not correct
- Timing/synchronization has been lost.

5.5.2   AAL Type 2

The AAL type 2 is proposed for VBR services with a timing relation between source and destination (class B, e.g. VBR audio or video). This type is not well defined yet. Therefore, most items are speculative.

5.5.2.1   Services and Functions

The AAL type 2 provides services to the adjacent higher layer which include the following features:

- Between the AAL and the higher layer, SDUs originating from a source with variable bit rate are interchanged.

- Timing information is transferred between source and destination.

- The higher layer is informed about errors (loss and misinsertion of cells) which cannot be corrected by the AAL.

Until now the following functions are defined which may be performed by the AAL to enhance the service provided by the ATM layer:

- Segmentation and reassembly of user information

- Handling of cell delay variation

- Handling of lost or misinserted cells

- Recovery of the source clock at the receiver

- Monitoring of the AAL-PCI for bit errors and handling of these errors

- Monitoring of the user information field for bit errors and possible corrective actions.

The allocation of these functions to CS and SAR as well as the need for additional functions need further study.

5.5.2.2   Segmentation and Reassembly Sublayer

The SAR accepts CS-PDUs with variable length and therefore it may be that a SAR-PDU cannot be fully filled.

The definition of the functions of the SAR, and of the SAR-PDU structure and its coding have not yet been completed.

In CCITT Recommendation I.363 [56], an example of a SAR-PDU is presented (see Figure 5.30). The need for the individual fields of this SAR-PDU has still to be assessed. Their position and their size are not yet fixed.

The use of the *sequence number* (SN) allows the detection of lost or misinserted cells. A specific value may be reserved for a specific purpose. The *information type* (IT) field may indicate *beginning of message* (BOM), *continuation of message* (COM) or *end of message* (EOM). It may also include some timing information or a discriminator for the components of audio or video signals. The *length indicator* (LI) is used for the indication of the number of CS-PDU octets carried in the SAR-PDU payload field. A *cyclic redundancy check* (CRC) protects the SAR-PDU against errors. The code to be chosen should be able to correct up to two correlated bit errors.

5.5.2.3   Convergence Sublayer

The CS may perform clock recovery for VBR audio and video services. This can be achieved by the insertion of a time stamp or a real-time synchronization word in the CS-PDU. The handling of lost or misinserted cells is also performed by the

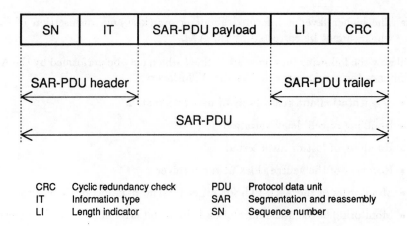

Figure 5.30: *Example SAR-PDU format for AAL type 2*

CS. If necessary, this sublayer may provide forward error correction capabilities for audio and video services.

5.5.2.4   Interaction with Other Planes

The AAL type 2 interacts with the management plane and the control plane. The information exchanged between the user plane of AAL type 2 and the management plane is identical to that exchanged between the user plane of AAL type 1 and the management plane (see Section 5.5.1.4).

5.5.3   AAL Type 3

Normally, the AAL type 3 is used for connection-oriented VBR services without any timing relation between source and destination (class C).

Only the SAR sublayer is described in this section because the CS is not yet defined.

5.5.3.1   Services

Two modes of service for AAL type 3 are defined. The *message mode service* can be used for framed data transfer (e.g. high level data link control frame) and the *streaming mode service* may be suitable for the transfer of low speed data with low delay requirements. The application of these modes to a particular service depends on the requirements of the service.

The message mode service provides the transport of a single AAL-SDU in one, or optionally more than one, CS-PDUs (see Figure 5.31).

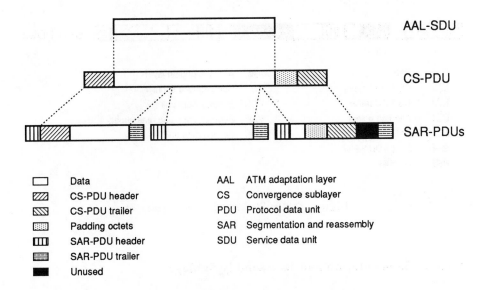

	Data	AAL	ATM adaptation layer
	CS-PDU header	CS	Convergence sublayer
	CS-PDU trailer	PDU	Protocol data unit
	Padding octets	SAR	Segmentation and reassembly
	SAR-PDU header	SDU	Service data unit
	SAR-PDU trailer		
	Unused		

Figure 5.31: *Message mode service*

In the streaming mode, one or more fixed-size AAL-SDUs are transported in one CS-PDU. The AAL-SDU may be as small as one octet and is always delivered as one unit, because only this unit will be recognized by the application (in one SAR-SDU, one AAL-SDU at most is contained). Figure 5.32 illustrates the operation of the streaming mode service.

Two peer-to-peer operation procedures are offered by both service modes:

Assured operation: The assured operation performs retransmission of missing or errored AAL-SDUs, and therefore flow control is provided as a mandatory feature. This operation mode may be restricted to point-to-point connections at the ATM layer.

Non-assured operation: In this mode, lost or errored AAL-SDUs will not be corrected by retransmission. The delivery of corrupted AAL-SDUs to the user may be provided as an optional feature. In principle, flow control can be applied to point-to-point ATM layer connections. For point-to-multipoint ATM layer connections, no flow control will be provided.

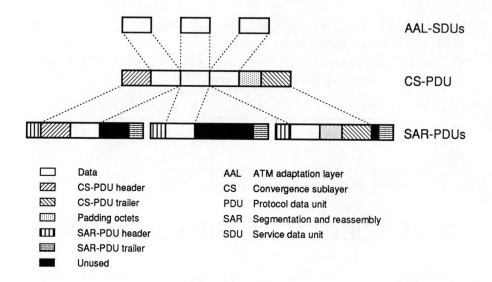

Figure 5.32: *Streaming mode service*

5.5.3.2   Segmentation and Reassembly Sublayer

In general the CS-PDUs have variable length. When accepting such a PDU the SAR sublayer generates SAR-PDUs containing up to 44 octets of CS-PDU data. The CS-PDU is preserved by the SAR sublayer. This requires a segment type indication and a SAR payload fill indication. The segment type indication identifies a SAR-PDU as being BOM, COM, EOM or single-segment message (SSM). The payload fill indication represents the number of octets of a CS-PDU contained in the SAR-PDU payload. In the case of the message mode service the SAR-PDU payload of all BOMs and COMs contains exactly 44 octets whereas the payload of EOMs and SSMs has variable length. In the streaming mode the SAR-PDU payload of all segments depends on the AAL-SDUs.

Error detection is the second function of the SAR sublayer. This function includes detecting bit errors in the SAR-PDU as well as detecting lost or misinserted SAR-PDUs. If one of these errors occurs, an indication will be sent to the CS.

The third function of the SAR sublayer may be the concurrent multiplexing/demultiplexing of CS-PDUs from multiple AAL connections over a single ATM layer connection. Further studies are necessary for evaluating the need of this function for AAL type 3.

To support all these functions, 4 octets are necessary (2 octets for the SAR-PDU header and 2 octets for the SAR-PDU trailer). Therefore, from the 48 octets of the

SAR-PDU, only 44 octets remain for the payload. In Figure 5.33 the SAR-PDU
format is depicted. The coding of this PDU conforms to the conventions and rules
described in Section 5.4.1.

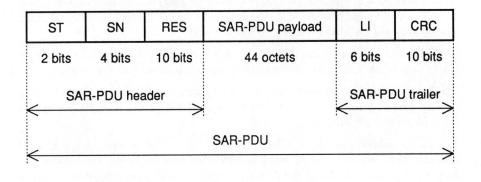

Figure 5.33: *SAR-PDU format for AAL type 3*

The *segment type* (ST) consists of 2 bits. Table 5.4 shows the association between
the meaning of the segment type and the coding of the ST field.

Segment Type	ST Field
BOM	10
COM	00
EOM	01
SSM	11

Table 5.4: *Coding of the segment type*

Four bits are available for the *sequence number* (SN) field. The SN of a SAR-PDU
is incremented by 1 relative to the SN of the previous SAR-PDU belonging to the
same AAL connection (numbering modulo 16).

The remaining 10 bits of the SAR-PDU header form the *reserved* (RES) field. In the future, this field may be used for multiplexing, but the need for that purpose or for other purposes is to be studied further. If the RES field is used for multiplexing different AAL connections on a single ATM layer connection, the AAL connections must have identical QOS characteristics. Multiplexing/demultiplexing will be on an end-to-end basis. The ATM layer connection which is used by different AAL connections will be administered as a single entity.

The SAR-PDU *payload* field (44 octets) is filled with CS-PDU data (left justified). If this field is not fully filled the remaining unused bits are coded as zero.

The *length indicator* (LI) field consists of 6 bits and contains the number of octets (binary coded) from the CS-PDU which are included in the SAR-PDU payload field. Its maximum value is 44.

The *cyclic redundancy check* (CRC) field (10 bits) is filled with the result obtained from a CRC calculation which is performed over the SAR-PDU header, the SAR-PDU payload field and the LI field. The following generating polynomial is proposed:

$$G(x) = x^{10} + x^9 + x^5 + x^4 + x + 1$$

The LSB of the result is right justified in the CRC field.

5.5.4   AAL Type 4

AAL type 4 primarily intends to support connectionless services (class D).

5.5.4.1   Services

The AAL type 4 provides the capabilities to transfer an AAL-SDU from one AAL user to one or more AAL users through the network using the service provided by the underlying ATM layer. Users will have the opportunity to select the appropriate AAL-SAP which will satisfy their QOS requirements.

The same modes of service and peer-to-peer operational procedures as described in Section 5.5.3.1 are available. However, the assured operation may not be necessary in a connectionless environment.

At each AAL-SAP the following two primitives together with their associated parameters are used:

1. AAL-UNITDATA-REQ (AAL-SAP-ID, DATA): This primitive requests the transfer of an AAL-SDU from the local AAL-entity to a single peer AAL-entity, or multiple peer AAL-entities.

2. AAL-UNITDATA-IND (AAL-SAP-ID, DATA, RECEPTION-STATUS):
This primitive indicates the delivery of an AAL-SDU from the AAL to the
AAL service user entity.

The DATA parameter specifies the AAL-SDU which will be exchanged across the
AAL-SAP. The AAL-SAP-ID has local significance which allows the AAL user
to select a specific AAL communication relation. The RECEPTION STATUS
indicates the success or failure of reception of an AAL-SDU. In the case of failure
the type will be indicated.

5.5.4.2   Segmentation and Reassembly Sublayer

The preservation of CS-PDU and error detection functions are identical to those
of the AAL type 3. For AAL type 4, multiplexing/demultiplexing of multiple CS-
PDUs concurrently over one ATM connection is well defined. For this purpose the
multiplexing identifier is used.

Figure 5.34 shows the format of a SAR-PDU for AAL type 4. The structure is
very similar to that of AAL type 3. Therefore, only the differences to AAL type
3 are described here.

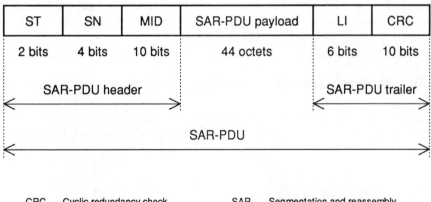

Figure 5.34: *SAR-PDU format for AAL type 4*

In the SAR-PDU for AAL type 4 the last 10 bits of the SAR-PDU header are used
as a *multiplexing identifier* (MID) field. SAR-PDUs with an identical MID belong

to a particular CS-PDU. The MID field assists in the interleaving of ATM-SDUs from different CS-PDUs and reassembly of these CS-PDUs.

5.5.4.3   Convergence Sublayer

The CS functions are performed per CS-PDU and depend on the applied service mode (message or streaming mode). The following functions are identified:

- Delineation of higher layer PDUs
- Mapping between AAL-SAPs and ATM layer connections
- Detection and handling of CS-PDU corruption and the optional discarding of these errored CS-PDUs
- The optional segmentation and reassembly of an AAL-SDU into two or more CS-PDUs for efficient transport across the ATM network
- Explicit indication of the information being carried within the CS-PDU
- The optional indication to the receiving peer entity of the maximum buffering requirements to receive the CS-PDU.

An example of a connectionless service is the *switched multi-megabit data service* (SMDS) [11] which is planned to be a high speed connectionless service that will extend LAN-like performance beyond the subscriber premises across the metropolitan area. SMDS is proposed to be on top of DQDB, however, an adapted version of the SMDS interface protocol (SIP) level 3 could be used as AAL CS protocol.

5.6   Higher Layers

In the previous sections the lower layers (physical layer, ATM layer, AAL) of the B-ISDN PRM were described. Aspects of higher layer protocols will be presented in this section.

5.6.1   User Plane

The higher layers of the user plane comprise all service-specific protocols which are necessary for the end-to-end communication. The higher layer protocols should be independent of the protocols used at the underlying layers.

In principle, existing higher layer protocols may be suitable. For some applications the existing higher layer protocols can be simplified because functions of higher layers are already performed by the ATM layer or the AAL. In other cases the extension of existing protocols may be necessary. In the long run, new optimized protocols may be developed to make the most efficient use of the ATM-based networks.

5.6.2   Control Plane

The control plane higher layers provide signalling message transport capabilities and connection/call control. In a first step (initial solution), these control functions at the B-ISDN UNI can be based on the existing protocols for user-network signalling [70, 71, 72, 73, 74, 75]. Some modifications will be necessary or advantageous, e.g.:

- Several layer 2 functions (cf. CCITT Recommendations Q.921 and Q.922 [71, 72]) are already provided by the ATM layer and the AAL (type 3 or 4) and need no longer be performed at layer 2. Addressing is done by means of VPI/VCI in the ATM layer and segmentation and reassembly are AAL functions.

- Layer 3 functions (cf. CCITT Recommendation Q.931 [74]) must be extended by new information elements for the characterization of ATM connections. In a first step, only the establishment and release of point-to-point VCCs is foreseen. To this aim at least allocation and identification of VCIs has to be realized. (VPC establishment can be done via ATM layer management procedures or even on subscription basis, therefore layer 3 support is not necessarily required.)

Similarly, inter-exchange signalling in the starting phase of B-ISDN can rely on the *common channel signalling system no. 7* (SS7) [69] that is being implemented for 64 kbit/s ISDN. Again, specific enhancements will be necessary to cater for ATM connections (e.g. VCI allocation/identification). For signalling transport the existing SS7 network can be used.

The target solution for signalling will be a completely revised protocol which should not only take into account broadband aspects but also upcoming non-broadband specific features like multi-media services or intelligent network capabilities (cf. Section 10.3).

5.7   Operation and Maintenance of the B-ISDN UNI

This section covers OAM of the user-network interface and the customer access controlled by the network. According to CCITT Recommendation I.610 [64] the minimum functions required to maintain the physical layer and the ATM layer of the customer access including the user-network interface are described. OAM of the layers above the ATM layer is not considered here.

First, the network configuration for OAM of the customer access is presented (Section 5.7.1). Then OAM functions of the physical layer and ATM layer and applications of the hierarchically structured OAM information flows – cf. Section

4.6.2 – are described (Section 5.7.2). In the last section (Section 5.7.3) implementation of these flows in the physical layer – flows F1, F2, F3 – and in the ATM layer – flows F4 and F5 – is shown.

5.7.1   Network Configuration for OAM of the Customer Access

The general arrangement for the maintenance of the customer access – based on the principles set out in CCITT Recommendation I.601 [63] – is given in Figure 5.35.

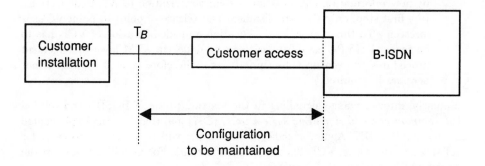

Figure 5.35: *Maintenance configuration of the customer access*

The customer installation in the above figure comprises a maintenance entity that communicates with the customer access maintenance centre located in the B-ISDN. Comprehensive general maintenance services are additionally available in the network to support maintenance of the customer access.

B-ISDN will make use of functions provided by the telecommunications management network (TMN) whose principles are described in CCITT Recommendation M.30 [66].

The architectural relation of the B-ISDN customer access with the TMN is shown in Figure 5.36.

The protocols used for maintenance are specified through Q interfaces. Results of network-element-internal monitoring will be delivered to the TMN via these Q interfaces.

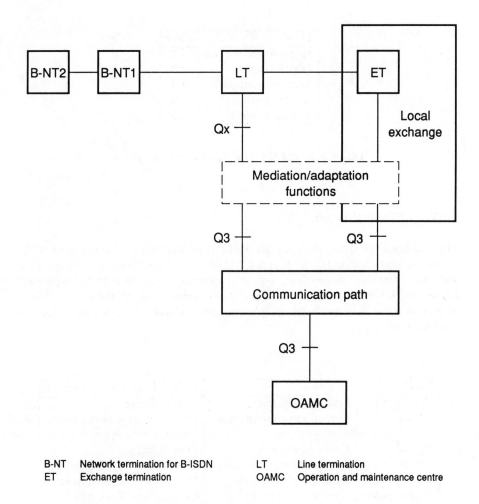

| B-NT | Network termination for B-ISDN | LT | Line termination |
| ET | Exchange termination | OAMC | Operation and maintenance centre |

Figure 5.36: *Possible TMN architecture for the customer access*

5.7.2 OAM Functions and Information Flows

In Figure 4.11 the hierarchical level structure of the physical layer and ATM layer and the corresponding information flows are shown. These levels and flows are summarized in Table 5.5.

Note that flows F1, F2, F3 belong to the physical layer, F4 and F5 to the ATM layer.

Level	Flow
Regenerator section	F1
Digital section	F2
Transmission path	F3
Virtual path	F4
Virtual channel	F5

Table 5.5: *OAM hierarchical levels and flows*

5.7.2.1   Physical Layer

Physical layer OAM functions are shown in Table 5.6. This table refers to SDH-based cell transmission (cf. Section 5.3.1.1). For cell-based transmission systems, some modifications are necessary, e.g. obviously there is no 'loss of AU-4 pointer' failure, so this item would be cancelled in the table. The SDH-function 'frame alignment' should be replaced by 'physical layer OAM cell recognition' for the cell-based option.

Level	Functions	Defect/Failure Detection
Regenerator section	Frame alignment	Loss of frame
	Section error monitoring	Degraded error performance (optional)
Digital section	Frame alignment	Loss of frame
	Section error monitoring	Degraded error performance
	Section error reporting	Degraded error performance
Transmission path	Customer network status monitoring	Customer network AIS
	Cell delineation	Loss of synchronization
	VC-4 offset	Loss of AU-4 pointer
	Header error performance monitoring	Degraded header error performance
	Path error monitoring	Degraded error performance
	Path error reporting	Degraded error performance
	Cell rate decoupling	Failure of insertion and suppression of idle cells

Table 5.6: *Physical layer OAM functions*

The first function shown in the table on the transmission path level requires some explanation. The status of the customer network will be continuously monitored, and in the case of transmission failure an *alarm indication signal* (AIS) will be generated.

AIS is a maintenance signal defined for the physical layer to indicate the detection and location of a transmission failure. AIS is applicable at both the section and path level. The same holds for the *far end receive failure* (FERF) signal (cf. Table 5.8 on page 110). The two signals serve the following purposes [62]:

> *AIS is used to alert the associated downstream termination point and connection point that an upstream failure has been detected and alarmed.*
> *FERF is used to alert the associated upstream termination point that a failure has been detected downstream.*

The AIS applied to the above mentioned customer network status monitoring is an F3 path AIS to protect, and provide failure information on, the transmission path between the B-NT2 and the path termination. Figure 5.37 shows the flows F1-F3 relating to physical layer OAM for different access configurations.

The upper part of the figure shows a customer directly connected with the local exchange. The transmission path (and the related F3 flow) extends between the B-NT2 and the exchange termination (ET). This path comprises the two sections between B-NT2 and B-NT1, and between B-NT1 and line termination (LT). Each of these sections is assigned an F2 flow. In the example given in the figure the second section comprises two regenerator sections with corresponding F1 flows. In the configuration shown in the middle of the figure the section starting at the B-NT1 is terminated by an LT in front of an STM multiplexer. Behind this STM multiplexer, another section begins. (Possible division of these sections into regenerator sections is not shown.) In the last configuration (lower part of the figure) a customer is connected with a VP cross-connect which terminates the transmission paths.

5.7.2.2 ATM Layer

OAM functions of the ATM layer are monitoring of VP availability and performance monitoring at VP and VC level (see Table 5.7).

The use of F4 and F5 flows is illustrated by an example in Figure 5.38.

The VPC maintained by means of F4 here extends between the B-NT2 and the ET, and the VCC extends between B-NT2 or a terminal and a termination point that may be, for example, the B-NT2 of another customer.

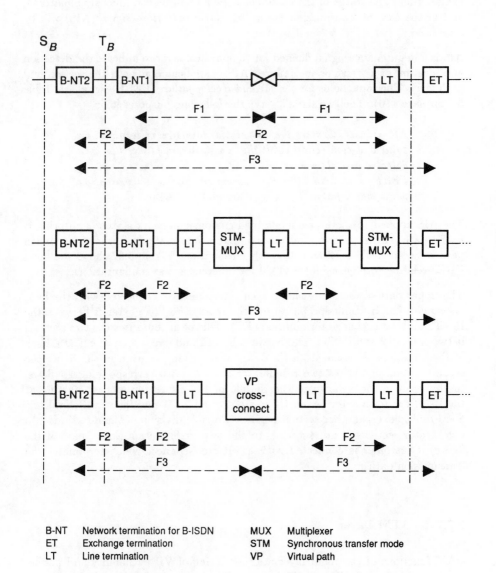

Figure 5.37: *Physical layer OAM flows*

Level	Functions	Defect/failure detection
Virtual path	Monitoring of path availability	Path not available
	Performance monitoring	Degraded performance
Virtual channel	Performance monitoring	Degraded performance

Table 5.7: *OAM functions of the ATM layer*

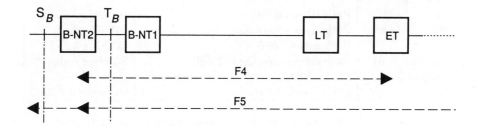

B-NT	Network termination for B-ISDN
ET	Exchange termination
LT	Line termination

Figure 5.38: *ATM layer OAM flows*

5.7.3   Implementation Issues

5.7.3.1   Physical Layer

Transmission overhead allocation and coding of the SDH physical layer functions as defined in Table 5.6 are given in Table 5.8 (cf. SDH frame structure, Section 5.3.1.1).

Transmission performance monitoring across the B-ISDN UNI in order to detect and report transmission errors will be performed at section and path level as indicated in Section 5.7.2.1.

At the SDH section level, an incoming signal is monitored at the section termination point by means of the BIP-24 that is inserted into the B2 field at the other

Octet	Function	Coding
STM-1 Section Overhead:		
A1	Frame alignment	11110110
A2	Frame alignment	00101000
B1	Regenerator section error monitoring[1]	BIP-8
B2	Section error monitoring	BIP-24
H1, H2	AU-4 pointer/path AIS	see [36]/all 1s
H3	Pointer action	see [36]
K2 (bits 6-8)	Section AIS/section FERF	111/110
Z2 (bits 18-24)	Section error reporting (FEBE)	B2 error count
VC-4 Path Overhead:		
J1	Path ID/verification	see [36]
B3	Path error monitoring	BIP-8
C2	Path signal label	'ATM cells'
G1 (bits 1-4)	Path error reporting (FEBE)	B3 error count
G1 (bit 5)	Path FERF[2]	1
H4	Cell offset indicator	see Section 5.3.1.1

[1] The use of B1 for regenerator section error monitoring across the B-ISDN UNI is application dependent and therefore optional.
[2] Path FERF should also be used to indicate loss of cell delineation.

Table 5.8: *SDH overhead allocation at the B-ISDN UNI*

section termination point.

The far end block error (FEBE) is used to perform the monitoring of an outgoing signal. This error count, obtained from comparing the calculated BIP-24 and the B2 value of the incoming signal at the far end, is inserted in the Z2 field bits 18-24 and then sent back, and it reports to the near end section termination point about the error performance of its outgoing signal as FEBE.

Similar to the SDH section level, at SDH path level, an incoming signal is monitored by using the BIP-8 of the B3 octet. Monitoring of an outgoing signal is performed using the path FEBE of bits 1-4 of the G1 octet. This concept is illustrated in Figure 5.39 (only the case 'A sending towards B' is shown for simplicity).

SDH as described in CCITT Recommendations G.708 [35] and G.709 [36] provides additional OAM means that will not necessarily be used in the customer access network. One example is automatic protection switching across the B-ISDN UNI. In the case of failure of the transmission line the system could automatically switch to a stand-by line to prevent longer out-of-order periods.

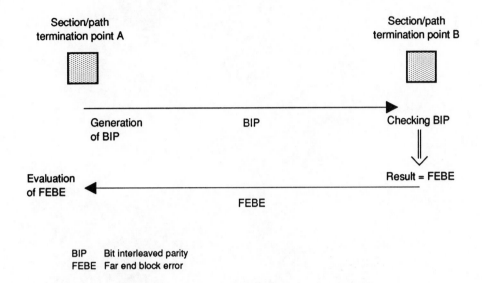

Figure 5.39: *Illustration of transmission performance monitoring*

5.7.3.2   ATM Layer

The ATM layer OAM flows F4 and F5 (cf. Table 5.7) are provided by cells dedicated to ATM layer OAM functions. This type of cell can be identified by specific values of the payload type identifier or VCI. F4 cells use a reserved VCI value and F5 cells a specific payload type identifier (these values are not yet defined).

Chapter 6

ATM Switching

Two main tasks can be identified for an ATM switching node or cross-connect node:

1. VPI/VCI translation

2. Cell transport from its input to its dedicated output.

To establish a connection between an arbitrary pair of inputs and outputs within a switching node, a switch fabric is necessary. In principle, a switch fabric can be implemented by a single switching element. Since such an element could not satisfy the requirements of a normal size ATM switching node, larger switch fabrics are used. These large switches are built up of switching elements.

The throughput of a switching node will be in the Gbit/s range and the cross-node delay as well as the cell loss should be kept very low. Therefore, no central control for the switching of cells can be applied. Only switch fabrics with highly parallel architectures can fulfil these stringent requirements.

6.1 Switching Elements

A *switching element* is the basic unit of a switch fabric. At the input port the routing information of an incoming cell is analysed and the cell is then directed to the correct output port. In general, a switching element consists of an interconnection network, an input controller (IC) for each incoming line and an output controller (OC) for each outgoing line (see Figure 6.1). In order to avoid excessive cell loss in the case of internal collisions (two or more cells compete for the same output simultaneously) buffers have to be provided within the switching element.

Arriving cells will be synchronized to the internal clock by the IC. The OC transports cells which have been received from the interconnection network towards the destination. ICs and OCs are coupled by the interconnection network.

113

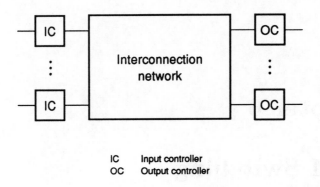

IC   Input controller
OC   Output controller

Figure 6.1: *General model of a switching element*

6.1.1   Matrix-Type Switching Elements

An internally non-blocking switching element will be achieved by using a rectangular matrix of cross-points for the interconnection network (see Figure 6.2). It is always possible to connect any idle input/output pair.

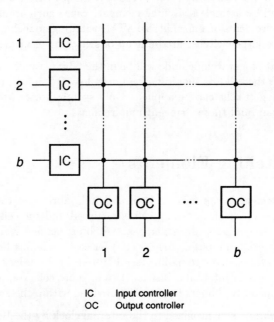

IC   Input controller
OC   Output controller

Figure 6.2: *Matrix-type switching element*

Different possibilities for the buffer location within this switching element exist [114, 132, 133]:

- Buffers are located at the input controllers
- Buffers are located at the output controllers
- Buffers are located at the cross-points.

6.1.1.1 Input Buffers

The cell buffers are located at the input controller (see Figure 6.3). When using first-in first-out (FIFO) buffers, a collision occurs if two or more head-of-the-queue cells compete simultaneously for the same output. Then all but one of the cells are blocked. The cells behind the blocked head-of-the-queue cell are also blocked even if they are destined for another, available output.

To overcome this disadvantage, FIFO buffers can be replaced by random access memories (RAMs) [135]. If the first cell in the buffer is blocked, the next cell which is destined for an idle output will be selected for transmission. However, this operation mode requires a more complex buffer control in order to find a cell destined for an idle output, and in order to guarantee the correct sequence of cells destined for the same output. The total buffer capacity will logically be subdivided in a load-dependent manner into single FIFOs (for each output one FIFO).

Further enhancements can be achieved if more than one cell can be transferred from one buffer to different outputs simultaneously. This requires a buffer with multiple outputs [119, 122] or a buffer with reduced access time.

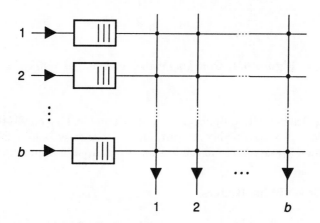

Figure 6.3: *Switching matrix with input buffers*

6.1.1.2   Output Buffers

Figure 6.4 shows a switching element which consists of a matrix with output buffers. Only if the matrix operates with the same speed as the incoming lines can collisions occur (several cells are hunting simultaneously for the same output). This drawback can be compensated by reducing the buffer access time and by a speed-up of the switching matrix. These factors may lead to technological limitations for the size of the switching element.

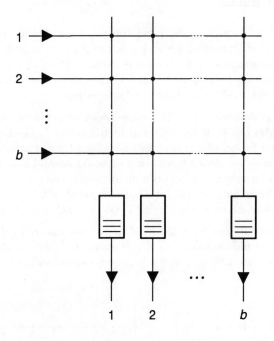

Figure 6.4: *Switching matrix with output buffers*

A switching element with output buffers will be non-blocking only if the speed-up factor is b for a $b \times b$ switching element. In all other cases, additional buffers at the input are necessary to avoid cell loss due to internal blocking.

6.1.1.3   Cross-Point Buffers

The buffers can also be located at the individual cross-points of the matrix (see Figure 6.5). This switching element is called a *Butterfly* switching element [21]. It avoids those cells hunting for different outputs influencing each other. If there are packets in more than one buffer belonging to the same output, a control logic has to choose the buffer which will be served first.

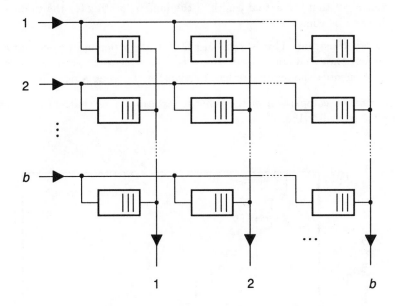

Figure 6.5: *Switching matrix with cross-point buffers*

From the performance point of view, this buffer location strategy has the drawback that at each cross-point a small buffer is required and no buffer sharing is possible. Therefore, the same efficiency that a switching element with output buffers provides cannot be achieved.

6.1.1.4 Arbitration Strategies

If several cells compete simultaneously for the same output, only one cell can be transferred and all other cells will be delayed. For the determination of the 'winning' cell, an arbitration strategy is required. Objectives for such a mechanism can be fairness or minimization of the cell loss, or minimization of the cell delay variations. The following strategies can be applied [106, 133]:

1. *Random*: The line which will be served first is chosen randomly among all lines competing for the same output. This strategy requires a small amount of implementation overhead.

2. *Cyclic*: The buffers are served in a cyclic order. This approach also requires only a small overhead.

3. *State dependent*: The first cell from the longest queue will be served first. For this algorithm the actual length of the buffers hunting for the same output have to be compared.

4. *Delay dependent*: This is a global FIFO strategy taking into account all the buffers that feed one output. However, this strategy implies some overhead to remember the relative order of arrival for the competing cells.

A performance comparison of the different arbitration mechanisms is shown in Figure 6.6 (see also [133]).

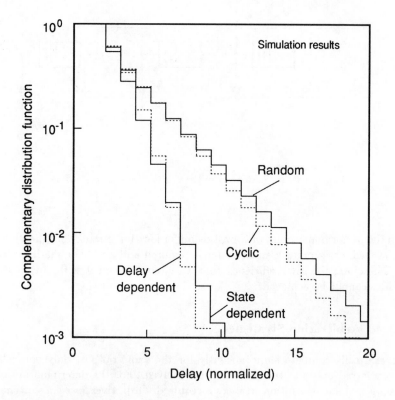

Figure 6.6: *Influences of the arbitration strategies on the delay*

The random strategy has the highest delay variations. An insignificant improvement can be yielded by using the cyclic strategy. The optimum strategy with respect to cell delay variation is the delay-dependent strategy. Minimum cell loss can be achieved by implementing the state-dependent algorithm. The performance with respect to the delay requirements of this strategy is slightly worse but still acceptable.

6.1.2 Central Memory Switching Element

The principle of a switching element with a central memory is depicted in Figure 6.7. All input and output controllers are directly attached to a common memory which can be written to by all input controllers and read by all output controllers.

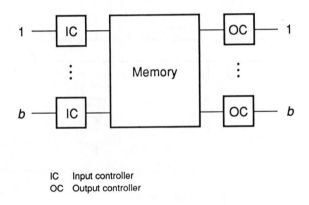

IC   Input controller
OC   Output controller

Figure 6.7: *Central memory switching element*

The best-known example of such an element has been used in the PRELUDE experiment [82]. The common memory can be organized to provide logical input as well as logical output buffers. Within the RACE project 1012 *Broadband Local Network Technology* the *Sigma* switch [96] is used which is based on a common memory structure with logical output buffers.

Since all buffers of the switching element share one common memory, significant reduction of the total memory requirements can be achieved in comparison with physically separated buffers. On the other hand, a high degree of internal parallelization is necessary in order to keep the frequency of memory access in a range of technological constraints.

6.1.3   Bus-Type Switching Element

The interconnection network can be realized by a high speed time division multiplexing (TDM) bus (see Figure 6.8). A conflict-free transmission can only be guaranteed if the total capacity of the bus is at least the sum of the capacities of all input links [85]. In order to achieve this high capacity, bit-parallel data transmission (e.g. 16 or 32 bit) on the bus system is required.

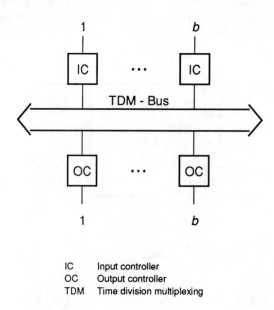

IC   Input controller
OC   Output controller
TDM   Time division multiplexing

Figure 6.8: *Bus-type switching element*

Normally, a bus access algorithm is applied which allocates the bus to the individual input controllers in constant intervals. Each input controller is able to transfer its cell towards the destination before the arrival of the next cell is completed. No buffers are required at the input controller. However, several cells may arrive at the same output controller whereas only one cell can leave the controller. Therefore, buffers are required at the output controller. This switching element yields the same performance as the matrix-type switching element with output buffers.

6.1.4 Ring-Type Switching Element

The ring-type switching element is shown in Figure 6.9. All input and output controllers are interconnected via a ring network which should be operated in a slotted fashion to minimize the overhead. In principle, a fixed time-slot allocation scheme can be used but this requires a ring capacity which is the sum of the capacities of all input links. If the ring capacity is less than the total input capacity, a flexible allocation scheme is necessary which results in an additional overhead.

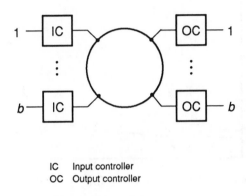

IC Input controller
OC Output controller

Figure 6.9: *Ring-type switching element*

The ring structure has the advantage over the bus structure in that a time-slot can be used several times within one rotation. However, this requires that the output controller empties a received time-slot. When using this destination release mechanism, an effective utilization of more than 100% can be achieved. This advantage has to be compared with the additional overhead for the destination release mechanism and the flexible time-slot allocation mechanism.

The ORWELL ring [2] is one approach for the implementation of a ring-type switching element. In order to fulfil the high throughput requirements, several rings are used in parallel forming a so-called torus of rings.

6.1.5 Performance Aspects

A lot of publications concerning performance comparisons of different buffering strategies exist [114, 122, 128, 132, 133]. Figure 6.10 (see also [133]) shows the mean cell delay of a 16 × 16 switching element with different buffer locations and buffer operation modes.

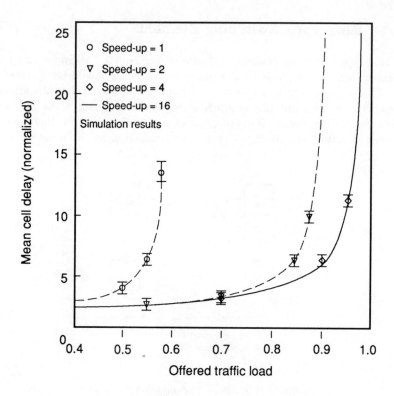

16 x 16 switching element with input and output buffers
Bernoulli arrival process

Figure 6.10: *Performance comparison of buffering strategies*

The results for the switching element with a simple FIFO input buffer correspond to the curve with speed-up factor 1. A speed-up factor i means that the buffer access time is reduced by the factor i or i cells from one buffer can be transferred simultaneously. The maximum throughput of this element is limited to about 58 % of the total capacity [114]. Good performance improvement will already be achieved using a speed-up factor of 2. The best results will be obtained for switching elements with a speed-up factor of 16. For this case the behaviour is identical to a switching element with output buffers. However, even with a speed-up factor of 4 [133] the ideal throughput can almost be obtained. This may result in a significant simplification of the implementation.

6.1.6   Technological Aspects

The performance results shown in Figure 6.10 are valid for infinite buffer size. However, as regards implementation, only finite buffer sizes are possible. Table 6.1 presents the buffer sizes (in cells) for switching elements of different size and different buffer locations assuming an average load of 85 % at each input and a permissible cell loss probability of 10^{-9} [122].

Type	Size	
	16×16	32×32
Central memory	113	199
Input buffer	320	640
Output buffer	896	1824

Table 6.1: *Buffer size requirements*

The central memory switching element requires lowest memory capacity due to the buffer sharing. The required memory capacity for a switching element with input buffers is low compared to the switching element with output buffers. This can be ascribed to the fact that in a switching element with input buffers only, one cell can be written into the buffer and several cells can be read from the buffer, whereas in the switching element with output buffers, several cells can simultaneously arrive but only one cell can leave.

In the following discussion it is assumed that a 16×16 or 32×32 switching element can be implemented in a single integrated circuit with complementary metal-oxide semiconductor (CMOS) or bipolar CMOS (BICMOS) technology. The chip area can be subdivided into the memory part and the random logic part (e.g. serial-to-parallel converter). In the central switching element the memory area is smallest whereas the required random logic area will be, without any doubt, larger than for the other two types.

Figure 6.11 shows the relationship between chip size and power dissipation for the three variants of switching elements. It must be pointed out that specific implementation principles and a certain type of CMOS technology were used. This is the reason why no scales are provided on the axes.

In CMOS technology the power dissipation of memories is very small. On the other hand, high speed random logic consumes a relatively high amount of power. This results in a non-linear relationship between chip size and power dissipation of the considered switching elements. From all these discussions it is evident that, concerning chip size and power dissipation, the central memory switching element

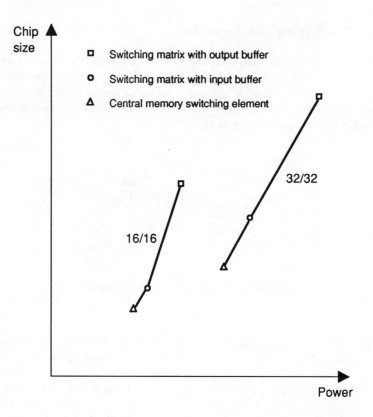

Figure 6.11: *Relationship between chip size and power dissipation*

has clear advantages, while the switching element with output buffers is the least favourable one.

6.2   Switching Networks

This section deals with the general classification of switching networks. Existing and proposed ATM-switch architectures of the individual manufacturers and research institutes will not be presented. A survey of various switches can be found in [3, 84, 121, 141].

Figure 6.12 gives an overview of the presented networks.

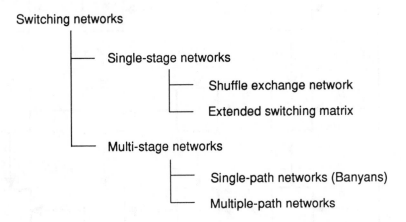

Figure 6.12: *Classification of switching networks*

6.2.1   Single-Stage Networks

A single-stage network is characterized by a single stage of switching elements which are connected to the inputs and outputs of a switching network.

6.2.1.1   Extended Switching Matrix

Figure 6.13 shows an example of an extended switching matrix which is formed from $b \times b$ switching elements. Basically, with this approach, each desired size of a switching network can be implemented.

For realizing the extended switching matrix the switching elements described in Section 6.1 have to be extended by additional b inputs and b outputs. Via the additional outputs the input signals are relayed to the next column of the matrix. The additional inputs are connected to the normal outputs of the switching element in the same column but in the row above.

The advantage of the extended switching element is the small cross-delay because cells will only be buffered once when crossing the network. It should be noted that the cross-delay is dependent upon the location of the input. The fact that the number of switching elements increases with the number of required inputs limits the size of an extended switching matrix. It is certainly possible to form such a single-stage network of the size 64 × 64 or 128 × 128, however, for larger systems, multi-stage networks will be preferred.

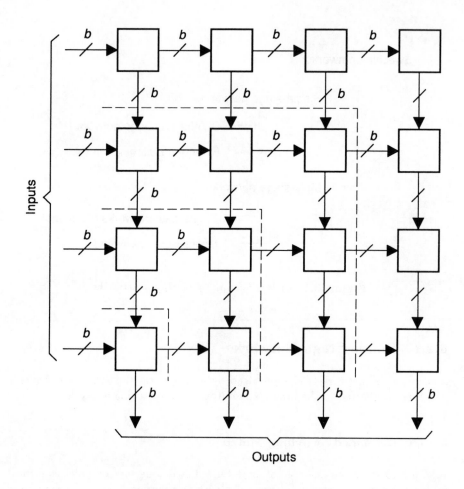

Figure 6.13: *Extended switching matrix*

6.2.1.2   Shuffle Exchange Network

The *shuffle exchange* network [81] is also a representative of the single-stage networks. It is based on a perfect shuffle permutation which is connected to a stage of switching elements (see Figure 6.14). In order to reach an arbitrary output from a given input, a feedback mechanism is necessary (dashed lines in Figure 6.14).

It is evident that a cell may pass the network several times before reaching its proper destination. Therefore, this network is also called a *recirculating* network. This type of network requires only a small number of switching elements but the performance is not very good.

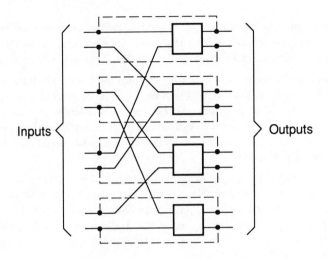

Figure 6.14: *Example of a shuffle exchange network*

6.2.2 Multi-Stage Networks

In order to avoid the drawbacks of the single-stage networks, multi-stage networks can be used. They are built of several stages which are interconnected by a certain link pattern. According to the number of paths which are available for reaching a destination output from a given input, these networks can be subdivided into two groups called *single-path* and *multiple-path* networks.

6.2.2.1 Single-Path Networks

In single-path networks, only one path exists for reaching the destination from a given input. These networks are also called *Banyan* networks [99]. Due to the fact that only one path exists for reaching the proper output, routing is very simple. Banyan networks have the disadvantage that internal blocking can occur. This results from the property that an internal link can be used simultaneously from different inputs. According to [106] Banyan networks can be classified into subgroups.

In *(L)-level* Banyan networks, only switching elements of adjacent stages are interconnected. Each path through the network passes exactly L stages. Furthermore, this class is subdivided into *regular* and *irregular Banyans*. Regular Banyans are constructed of identical switching elements whereas in irregular Banyans different types of switching elements can be used. The *generalized delta* network [87] belongs to the class of irregular Banyans.

Regular Banyans have the advantage that they can be implemented economically because they are constructed of identical switching elements. In the following, only *SW-Banyans*, which are a subclass of the regular Banyans, will be considered.

SW-Banyans can be constructed recursively from the basic switching element with F input links and S output links. The simplest SW-Banyan is a single switching element (called (1)-level Banyan). An (L)-level SW-Banyan will be obtained by connecting several $(L-1)$-level SW-Banyans with an additional stage of $(F \times S)$ switching elements. These extra switching elements are connected in a regular manner to the SW-Banyans.

Delta networks [129] are a special implementation of SW-Banyans. L-level networks which are constructed of $(F \times S)$ switching elements have S^L outputs. Each output can be identified by a unique destination address which is a number of base S with L digits. Each digit specifies the destination output of the switching element in a specific stage. This allows a simple routing of cells through the delta network which is called *self-routing*.

In *rectangular delta* networks the switching elements have the same number of inputs and outputs $(S = L)$. Consequently, the number of network inputs is equal to the number of network outputs. These networks are also called delta-S networks. Figure 6.15 shows a delta-2 network with four stages which has the topology of a *baseline* network [146]. The thick line indicates the path from input 5 to output 13 (binary destination address 1101).

Bidelta networks are a special class of delta networks. They remain delta networks even if the inputs are interpreted as outputs and vice versa. All bidelta networks are topologically equivalent and can be transformed into each other by renaming the switching elements and the links [87].

6.2.2.2   Multiple-Path Networks

In multiple-path networks, a multiplicity of alternative paths exist for reaching the destination output from a given input. This property has the advantage that internal blocking can be reduced or even avoided.

During the connection set-up phase in most multiple-path networks the internal path will be determined and all cells of the connection will use the same internal path. If FIFOs are provided in the individual switching elements, cell sequence integrity can be guaranteed and no resequencing is necessary.

In this classification, multiple-path networks will be subdivided into *folded* and *unfolded* networks.

Figure 6.16 shows a three-stage folded network. In folded networks, all inputs and outputs are located at the same side of the switching network and the network's internal links are operated in a bidirectional manner (each link drawn in Figure 6.16 represents the physical lines for both directions).

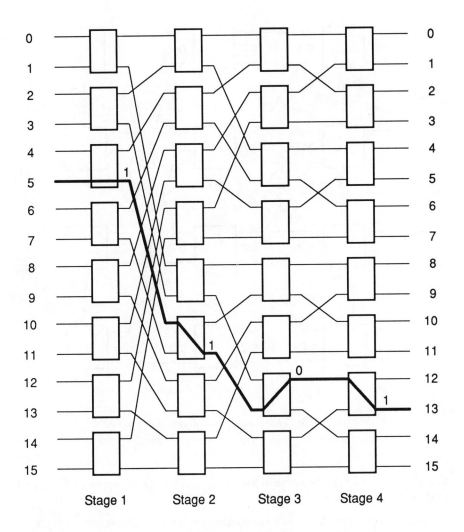

Figure 6.15: *Delta-2 network with four stages*

Folded networks have the advantage that *short* paths [122, 140] can be used; e.g. if the input line and the output line are connected to the same switching element, cells can be reflected at the switching element and need not be passed to the last stage (reflection stage). The number of switching elements that the cells of a connection have to pass depends on the location of the input and output lines.

The port capacity of a three-stage folded network built up from $b \times b$ switching elements is $(b/2)(b/2)b$. With today's technologies, switching elements of size

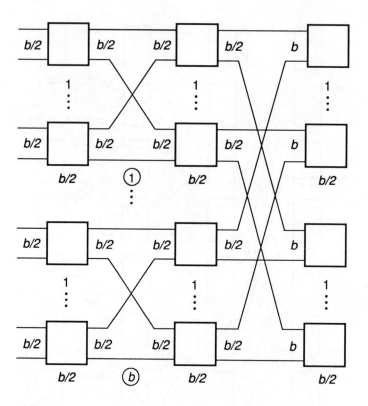

Figure 6.16: *Three-stage folded switching network*

16×16 and 32×32 can be realized leading to three-stage networks with 1024 and 8192 ports, respectively.

In unfolded networks the inputs are located on the one side and the outputs on the opposite side of the network. The internal links are unidirectional and all cells have to pass the same number of switching elements.

Multiple-path unfolded network structures will be based on single-path network structures. Again, the basis for these networks are $b \times b$ switching elements. For simplicity, only 2×2 switching elements are presented in the figures.

In [142] a switching network is described which consists of a buffered Banyan network and a preceding *distribution network* (see Figure 6.17). The distribution network has the purpose of distributing cells as evenly as possible over all inputs of the Banyan network. With this approach, internal blocking can be reduced. However, the cell sequence integrity of a connection cannot be maintained and therefore an additional resequencing mechanism is required at the output.

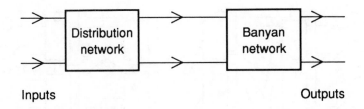

Figure 6.17: *Basic structure of a distribution/Banyan network*

Another possibility for the realization of such networks is the use of a *sorting net-work* [10] and a *trap network* in front of a Banyan network [105] (see Figure 6.18). The sorting network arranges arriving cells in a monotonous sequence depending on the network internal destination address. Cells with identical addresses are detected by the trap network and all but one of these cells are fed back to the input of the sorting network. Cells which have to pass the sorting network again will get higher priority in order to maintain cell sequence integrity. All cells arriving at the Banyan network can be transported to their destination without any internal blocking.

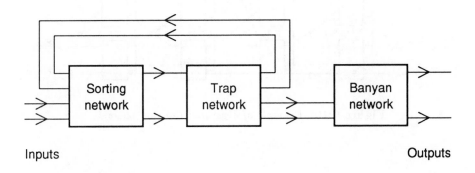

Figure 6.18: *Basic structure of a sorting/trap/Banyan network*

Multiple-path networks can also be realized by using several planes of Banyan networks in parallel (see Figure 6.19). This is called *vertical stacking* [120].

All cells belonging to the same connection will pass the same plane. This will be determined during the connection set-up phase. An incoming cell will be switched to its appropriate plane by the distribution unit which is located at each input line. At the switch output, a statistical multiplexer collects cells from all planes.

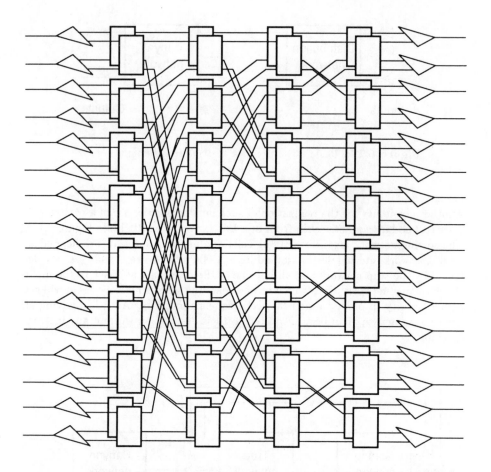

Figure 6.19: *Example of a parallel Banyan network*

In [140] it is shown that even with two planes in parallel a virtually non-blocking switching structure can be achieved.

Adding a number of stages to a given Banyan network is called *horizontal stacking* [120]. A *multi-path interconnection network* (MIN) [4] is realized by adding a baseline network with reversed topology to an existing baseline network (see Figure 6.20). The baseline network has already been presented in Figure 6.15.

Assuming $b \times b$ switching elements the $N \times N$ network has $2 \log_b N$ stages. In an $N \times N$ network, N internal paths are available to reach a given output from an arbitrary input. From a particular input the internal path can be selected arbitrarily until the output of the baseline network is reached. Then the way

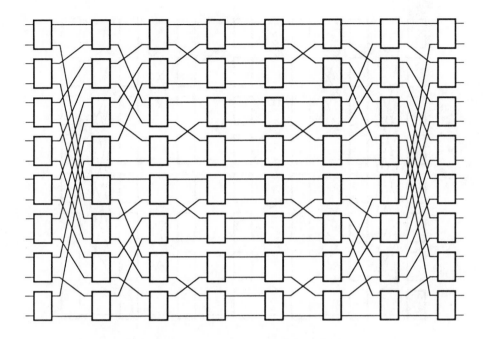

Figure 6.20: *Example of a multi-path interconnection network*

through the reversed baseline network is fixed.

A Beneš network [13] is very similiar to a MIN. The difference is that the last stage of the baseline network coincides with the first stage of the reversed baseline network. Therefore, the number of stages is reduced by 1 compared with the MIN. Figure 6.21 shows a seven-stage Beneš network.

Again, assuming $b \times b$ switching elements, only N/b alternative paths are available for reaching any output from any input. Each path is uniquely determined by the switching element passed in the centre stage.

6.2.3 Cell Header Processing in Switch Fabrics

The main tasks of ATM switching nodes are:

1. VPI/VCI translation

2. Transport of cells from the input to the appropriate output.

In order to fulfil these tasks, two approaches can be applied [136]:

- *Self-routing principle*

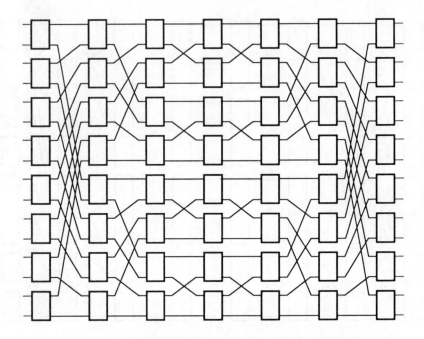

Figure 6.21: *Example of a seven-stage Beneš network*

- *Table-controlled principle.*

6.2.3.1   Self-Routing Switching Elements

When using self-routing switching elements the VPI/VCI translation only has to be performed at the input of the switching network. After the translation the cell is extended by a switching network internal header. This header precedes the cell header. The cell header extension requires an increased network internal speed.

In a network with k stages the internal header is subdivided into k subfields. Subfield i contains the destination output number of the switching element in stage i. Figure 6.22 shows the cell header processing in a switching network built up of self-routing switching elements.

6.2.3.2   Table-Controlled Switching Elements

When using the table-controlled principle the VPI/VCI of the cell header will be translated in each switching element into a new one. Therefore, the cell length need

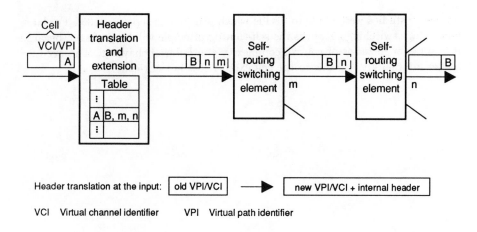

Figure 6.22: *Self-routing switching elements*

not be altered. Figure 6.23 shows the header processing in a switching network which consists of table-controlled switching elements.

During the connection set-up phase the contents of the tables are updated. Each table entry consists of the new VPI/VCI and the number of the appropriate output.

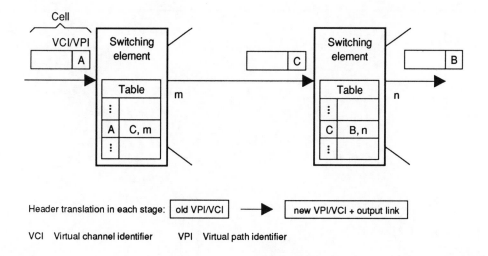

Figure 6.23: *Table-controlled switching elements*

Extensive studies were made to decide which principle is superior [136]. For large multi-stage switching networks the self-routing principle will be preferred because it is superior in terms of control complexity and failure behaviour. The need for higher internal bit rate due to the cell extension is not critical.

Chapter 7

ATM Transmission Network

In Sections 4.1 and 4.2.1, general network aspects of the ATM-based B-ISDN were addressed. One main feature of an ATM network is the establishment of VCCs and VPCs as described in Section 4.2.1. Switching of ATM cells has already been treated in Chapter 6. In the present chapter, transmission aspects of ATM networks are discussed. After a brief overview of network elements like ATM multiplexers and cross-connects, transmission systems for ATM cell transport and network synchronization will be discussed. Emphasis will be put on possible local loop implementations.

7.1   Overview

7.1.1   Cell Transfer Functions

The transfer of cells through an ATM network is supported by the following functions:

- Generation of cells (packetizer, or more precisely, ATM-izer, e.g. in a B-ISDN terminal)

- Transmission of cells

- Multiplexing/concentrating of cells

- Cross-connecting of cells

- Switching of cells.

ATM cell switching has been studied in Chapter 6. Cell transmission will be addressed in Section 7.1.2, while the other functions will be discussed in this section.

7.1.1.1   Generation of Cells

A B-ISDN terminal will send all its information mapped into cells (besides transmission overhead in the SDH option, cf. Section 5.3.1.1), therefore, no additional packetizing function is required in the ATM network in this case.

Packetizers will be required, however, whenever interworking with non-ATM equipment has to be performed. An ATM packetizer either cuts STM channels into pieces suitable to fit the ATM cell format or adapts non-ATM packets to ATM cells. Such signal conversion may be required at the B-NT2 (see Section 5.2.4) which can provide the user with ATM interfaces and non-ATM interfaces as well, or at any other place in the network where connection of non-ATM traffic is to be foreseen (e.g. in an ATM multiplexer or switch). The reverse procedure (depacketizing) has of course to be performed when ATM traffic is converted to non-ATM type traffic.

The use of ATM cell packetizers in a customer network is depicted in Figure 7.1. Figure 7.2 shows applications of ATM cell packetizers in the public network.

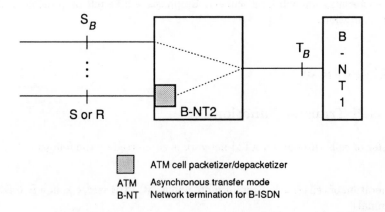

Figure 7.1: *The use of cell packetizers/depacketizers in the customer network*

The need to convert non-ATM signals to ATM cell format will especially arise in the introductory phase of ATM networks (see Chapter 8).

The problems due to packetization delay for ATM speech connections will be discussed in Section 9.2.

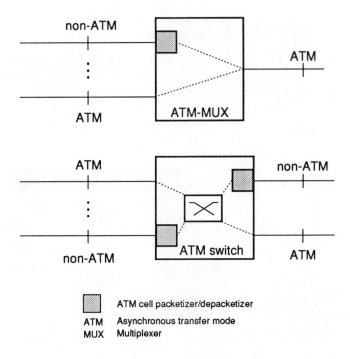

Figure 7.2: *The use of cell packetizers/depacketizers in the public network*

7.1.1.2   Multiplexing/Concentration of Cells

Figure 5.37 showed the use of a STM multiplexer which multiplexes several signals originating from different B-ISDN customers on to a single access line. In this STM-type multiplexer, no (cell) concentration takes place, i.e. idle cells will not be removed as the STM multiplexer does not process the signal payload carrying ATM cells. A simple example is shown in Figure 7.3.

In an ATM multiplexer, all incoming idle cells will be sorted out. Thus, the ATM traffic can be concentrated. The achievable degree of concentration depends on the traffic characteristics and the requested quality of service. An example where an ATM multiplexer is deployed is shown in Figure 7.4, where customers share a common 155.520 Mbit/s access line.

The ATM multiplexer unpacks arising ATM cells from the transmission frame (in the figure the SDH STM-1 frame is indicated), eliminates idle cells (and erroneous, incorrectable ones) and multiplexes the valid cells into one STM-1 frame. In this example the ratio of the gross bit rates at both sides of the multiplexer is $1/m$. This can only work if m is a small number (e.g. m up to 8) and the maximum sum

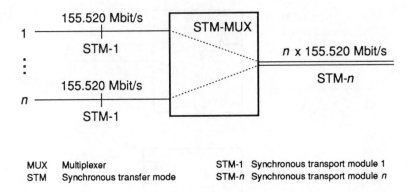

MUX   Multiplexer   STM-1 Synchronous transport module 1
STM   Synchronous transfer mode   STM-*n* Synchronous transport module *n*

Figure 7.3: *STM multiplexer*

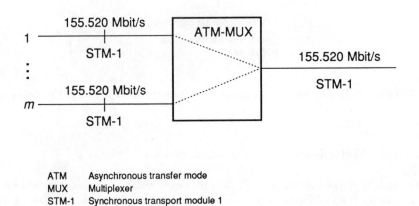

ATM   Asynchronous transfer mode
MUX   Multiplexer
STM-1 Synchronous transport module 1

Figure 7.4: *Example of an ATM multiplexer*

bit rate used at any time by any tributary is small compared with 155.520 Mbit/s, i.e. does not exceed about, say, 20 - 30 Mbit/s.

7.1.1.3   Cross-Connecting of Cells

An ATM cross-connect is a VP switch that can flexibly map incoming VPs on to outgoing VPs and thus enable establishment of VPCs through the ATM network. The cross-connect also concentrates ATM traffic as it eliminates idle cells.

(Morever, it performs necessary OAM functions of the physical layer and the ATM layer as does the ATM multiplexer.)

A cross-connect can be used, for example, in the access network to separate customer traffic that is destined for the local switch from that to be transmitted on a fixed route through the network to a fixed endpoint (see Figure 7.5).

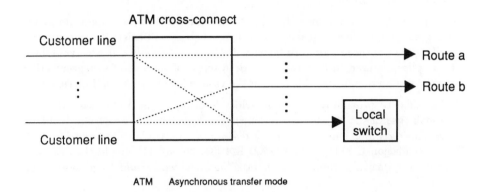

Figure 7.5: *ATM cross-connect*

7.1.2 Transmission Systems

ATM cells can in principle be transported on many transmission systems. The only requirement is that bit sequence independence is guaranteed so that there are no restrictions on allowed cell information contents.

For the user-network interface at S_B and T_B reference points, two options have been defined, one based on SDH and the other on pure cell multiplexing (see Section 5.2.3). In the network, other transmission systems may also be used. One example is the PDH as recommended in CCITT Recommendation G.703 [33]. PDH provides gross bit rates of about 2, 34, 140 Mbit/s or 1.5 and 45 Mbit/s (these two branches of hierarchical levels are used, for example, in Europe and in North America, respectively). In the introductory phase of B-ISDN, some countries want to employ existing transmission systems like PDH to support ATM cell transport.

7.1.3 Network Synchronization

An ATM transport network needs bit timing and cell timing. At any entrance point of an ATM multiplexer or ATM switch, an individual synchronizer is provided that adapts cell timing of the incoming signal to the internal timing. Transmission links therefore in principle need not be synchronized with each other. Each synchronizer can adjust differing phases in units of a cell (idle cell stuffing/extraction). When limiting the maximally tolerable distance between two subsequent idle cells (e.g. 256 cells), a certain frequency deviation of the link clock from the internal clock can be handled. The above considerations show that an ATM network basically need not be synchronous.

However, ATM networks must be able to integrate STM-based applications including audio and video transmission as long as those will exist. To this aim the sampling clock of the sender must be provided to the receiver in order to avoid slips. This implies requirements on the network in terms of support of synchronization of the access lines and tolerable slips in the case of synchronization failure.

One method to provide the necessary clock information in ATM-based B-ISDN is to make use of the existing clock distribution network for the 64 kbit/s ISDN. Performance requirements on the clock distribution network according to CCITT Recommendation G.811 [37] and G.821-824 [38, 39, 40, 41] should then be considered as a basis for discussion on broadband networks and, if necessary, be redefined.

The derivation of the B-ISDN clock from the 64 kbit/s ISDN clock distribution network is shown in Figure 7.6.

The 64 kbit/s ISDN is structured into several hierarchical levels (in the figure, four levels are indicated, as is the case in Germany). Each node receives its clock from the node of the higher level, the highest level node deriving its timing directly from the clock distribution network. In the case of failure, stand-by connections can be used to derive timing via alternative paths.

The simplest implementation for B-ISDN could be to derive timing of each node from the corresponding 64 kbit/s ISDN node as shown in the figure (here, too, stand-by timing connections are foreseen to cover failure situations). Note that B-ISDN will most probably have fewer hierarchical levels than the 64 kbit/s ISDN. As clock accuracy decreases when going down to lower levels, it may become necessary to derive the clock for B-ISDN not from the corresponding 64 kbit/s ISDN level but from a higher one (or even directly from the clock distribution network).

7.1.3.1   Synchronization of Terminals

For a constant bit rate service the source sampling frequency f_s and the filling rate R_c of cells pertaining to this service are tightly correlated:

$$R_c = f_s/48$$

(The ATM cell information field has 48 bytes.)

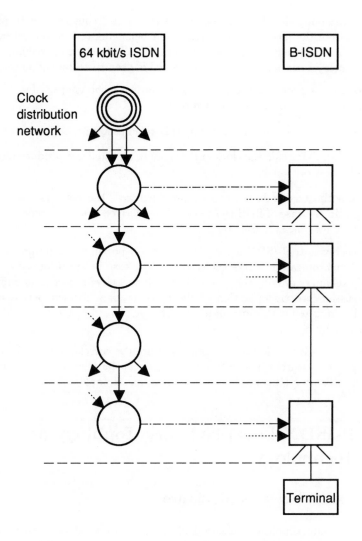

Figure 7.6: *Example of network synchronization for B-ISDN*

So at the receiving side the original source sampling frequency can in principle be derived from the rate of those arriving cells belonging to the connection under consideration. However, due to the nature of the ATM network, arriving cells are subject to delay variation whose compensation is deemed to be not so easy.

To overcome this problem, a STM-like mechanisn can be adopted for ATM networks on an end-to-end basis provided that:

- timing of the sending side (terminal) is synchronized with network timing

- at the receiving side the clock of the sending terminal is reproduced by virtue of the network clock.

To this aim the terminals have to be provided with the network clock via the access line. In the case of SDH the clock will be derived from the signal across the user-network interface (cf. Section 5.3.2.2).

In the synchronous B-ISDN shown in Figure 7.6 no slips can occur as long as network synchronization works correctly. In the case of synchronization failure the local exchanges provide the access lines with a clock of an accuracy sufficiently high to sustain orderly operation of the accesses for a defined period of time. Terminals connected with different local exchanges must be able to get rid of slips which then may occur.

In a synchronous network, source signals that are not correlated with the network clock (e.g. video-sources in free-running mode) can be transmitted by means of positive justification (this method is described, for example, in [17]).

7.2   B-ISDN Local Network Topology and Technology

7.2.1   Local Network Structure

The conceptually simplest realization of the B-ISDN local network is the star topology where there is one access line per customer. The remaining problem to be solved could then be to define the characteristics of the digital section extending between T_B and V_B reference points (see Figure 7.7 (a)).

For the B-ISDN local network, however, other structures are also being investigated as candidates for implementation. These are, for example, multiple star, ring, bus and tree configurations. Some examples are depicted in Figure 7.7. Case (b) shows the multiple star configuration where several customers' signals are multiplexed on to one access line. Optionally, there might be an additional cross-connect to provide different paths through the network. Its functionality may comprise:

(a) **Star configuration**

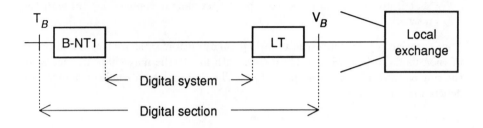

(b) **Multiple star configuration**

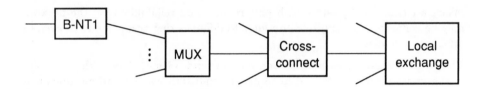

(c) **Ring configuration**

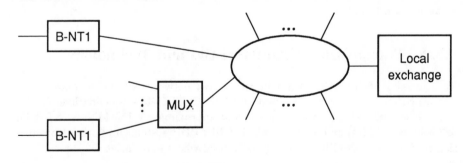

B-NT1   Network termination 1 for B-ISDN
LT   Line termination
MUX   Multiplexer

Figure 7.7: *Examples of local network structures*

- connection of customers with big traffic volumes directly to the local exchange

- separating traffic that is to be switched in the local exchange from the traffic that is to be routed on a fixed path (permanent connection) through the network.

Configuration (c) is a ring structure where many customers share a common transmission medium (e.g. MAN). Customers with low traffic may share the access to the ring as shown in the lower part of (c). The ring may be a single or double ring depending on:

- number and location of customers

- throughput requirements

- availability criteria

- cost aspects.

When a customer requests a high performance and reliability level the network may be connected via multiple interfaces to different ring access nodes or even to different exchanges.

The ring structure saves transmission lines in terms of metres of cable to be laid in the ground but is restricted in terms of bandwidth available to an individual user and in terms of upgradability (the same holds for bus configurations). In a star or multiple star configuration it is easier to connect additional customers to the B-ISDN.

Tree configurations will be discussed later in connection with B-ISDN introduction scenarios (see Chapter 8).

7.2.2   Transmission Characteristics and Technology

Transmission of B-ISDN signals in the access network will be predominantly performed via optical systems based on SDH (CCITT Recommendations G.707-709 [34, 35, 36]) which provide bit rates of approximately 155 Mbit/s (STM-1), 622 Mbit/s (STM-4) and 2.5 Gbit/s (STM-16). PDH systems and other transmission media (e.g. radio links) could also be used where appropriate.

Use of single-mode fibres according to CCITT Recommendation G.652 [31] is favoured in the access network as this allows longer distances to be covered. Optical signals can be generated by laser diodes. The electronic parts will be based on CMOS technology for bit rates up to 155 Mbit/s and on bipolar technology for higher bit rates.

Two optical fibres (one for each direction of transmission) may be employed, or alternatively optical wavelength division multiplexing (WDM) on one single fibre to separate both transmission directions by different wavelengths (e.g. 1530 nm and 1300 nm). Later, a more advanced technology like coherent multi-channel transmission will possibly be employed (cf. Chapter 10).

The bit error probability of the optical transmission link should be less than 10^{-9}. An ATM switch will guarantee a cell loss probability of about 10^{-9} (cf. Section 6.1.6). Cell loss in an ATM switch is primarily caused by buffer overflow in the case of traffic congestion or detection of uncorrectable errors in the cell header. If the transmission bit error probability is less than 10^{-9}, the latter effect is negligibly small as it requires the occurrence of specific multiple-bit errors in one cell header.

7.2.2.1 Maintenance Aspects of Optical Transmission

The following failures may occur in optical transmission systems:

- Laser light emission failure
- Laser sends continuous 1s
- Receiver indicates continuous 0s or 1s.

In the case of such a failure the corresponding message will be delivered to a line maintenance entity (usually located in the local exchange) which is responsible for setting the appropriate alarms, i.e. urgent alarm in the case of a unit out of order and warning in the case of a unit exhibiting deteriorioated performance.

7.3 Trunk Network Structure

A possible trunk network implementation is shown in Figure 7.8. (Realization of internodal signalling connections is not discussed in this chapter. Signalling may be established via the existing SS7 routes or, in the long run, over the ATM network itself.)

In Figure 7.8 the following network elements are visualized:

- B-ISDN exchange (VC/VP switch)
- ATM cross-connect (VP switch)
- STM multiplexer/cross-connect.

The ATM cross-connects act as VP switches and can flexibly provide VP connections through the network (cf. Section 4.2). STM cross-connects may be deployed in addition to facilitate rearrangement of physical paths, e.g. in the case of transmission failures (protection switching). Finally, STM multiplexers merge, for example, 155.520 Mbit/s STM-1 signals into the higher bit rate signals STM-4 or STM-16 of about 622 Mbit/s or 2.5 Gbit/s, respectively.

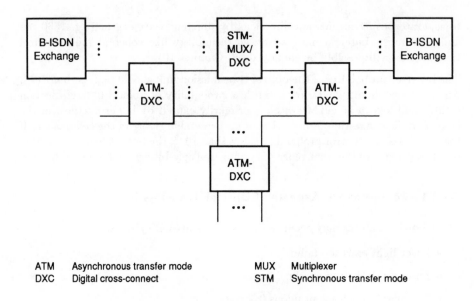

ATM	Asynchronous transfer mode
DXC	Digital cross-connect

MUX	Multiplexer
STM	Synchronous transfer mode

Figure 7.8: *Example of trunk network structure*

ATM cross-connects process each arriving cell; according to its VPI value, a cell is routed into the direction that is defined by the associated VPC. Therefore, VPCs with arbitrary bit rates can be established and switched through an ATM cross-connect. Establishment and release of VPCs can in principle be initiated by the user or the network provider by means of, for example, ATM layer management or – probably in a later stage – signalling procedure. The time required for establishment or release of VPCs will be much shorter than the realization of the request for a reserved, permanent channel in today's networks, i.e. VPC establishment can be performed within a couple of seconds. The same time scale applies to the automatic rearrangement of SDH paths in the case of transmission failures (protection switching).

Multiplexers and cross-connects can be used to decouple the logical point-to-point configuration of the ATM switching network from the actual topology of the fibre-based transmission network and to achieve:

- flexibility concerning realization of hierarchically structured networks or networks with any other structure (e.g. meshed rings)

- easy provision of additional network capacity in the case of growing traffic

- a means to be able to offer required redundancy for ATM connections between exchanges.

Segregation of ATM traffic with low/medium bit rates per connection from ATM traffic with high bit rates in the trunk network may help to manage ATM traffic more efficiently.

Individual channels with the same destination can be grouped to be carried on the same VP. Transit nodes of the ATM network act as VP switches with pre-established (redundant) VPC capabilities between the B-ISDN exchanges and need not handle VC switching. This alleviates operation of transit nodes especially in the case of many simultaneous low bit rate connections on a trunk line.

Chapter 8

Evolution Scenarios for B-ISDN

B-ISDN, being based on

- optical fibre transmission

- asynchronous transfer mode (i.e. a new switching and networking concept)

- new service categories (e.g. multi-media services involving video)

- and, last but not least, new network features like *intelligent network* (IN) and *telecommunications management network* (TMN) that are conceptually not tied to B-ISDN but will most probably be implemented in a future network like B-ISDN

is obviously a challenging task for network providers and manufacturers as well. Its acceptance by potential customers requires a careful introduction strategy and evolution concept.

'Despite the convincing advantages of this universal broadband ISDN for all services, the high development and investment costs mean that it cannot in the short or medium term achieve wide coverage. The aim must therefore be to expand and add to the present-day telecommunication networks – of these primarily the network with most subscribers of all, the telephone network – in a market and demand-oriented manner with suitable technical concepts and in timed phases, thereby achieving a gradual transition to the ubiquitous, multi-subscriber network of the future. Any intended individual solutions or intermediate solutions must be designed such that they can later be incorporated with the least possible expense in the intelligent integrated broadband network' [138].

As the existing telecommunication network structures differ from country to country and the customers' needs also differ, there cannot be a single valid evolution path towards B-ISDN all over the world. So necessarily all evolution scenarios are only examples whose steps may shed some light on the development characteristics of networks towards B-ISDN but may not be taken as a straightforward implementation plan for B-ISDN that would be viable in every country.

151

Introduction and evolution towards B-ISDN must in any case consider the strong need to interwork with existing services and networks, e.g. telephony, 64 kbit/s ISDN, data (packet) networks and TV distribution networks. So in the following the interworking with, and in a later phase the integration of, such services and networks will be addressed. In the opinion of most market experts the era of broadband (public) networks will be ushered in with fast data services that are requested by business customers. To support currently installed customer networks (LANs etc.) which are usually run with connectionless protocols the future B-ISDN will have to offer connectionless service capabilities (as discussed in Section 9.1) from the beginning. This aspect will be described in Section 8.4.

A quite different introduction scenario foresees provision of optical fibres to the homes of residential customers (cf. Sections 8.1 - 8.3) who might above all be interested in entertainment programmes. Interactive services in addition to plain telephony may gradually be offered according to the customers' wishes.

8.1   Fibre to the Customer

The demand for broadband services will develop only gradually, and 'it therefore seems advisable if the introduction of fibre optic technology for the subscriber access is not coupled firmly to new interactive broadband services. Instead, solutions are initially needed whereby optical fibres can be economically brought as close as possible to the subscriber, also for already existing services (television, telephony, data transfer)' [138].

Thus, the magic spell is *fibre to the office* or *fibre to the home*, respectively. In the case of business customers with large or at least quickly expanding traffic volumes, it may already pay for network providers to install individual optical fibre lines. Due to their vast transmission capacity, they are deemed to be a future-proof investment. In the case of residential customers the hope for quick returns is not so justified. So in this case, resource-sharing concepts have to be considered in order to be able to be cost-effective.

One of those concepts is the passive optical network (PON) (cf. [92]). A single fibre from the exchange feeds a number of customers via passive optical branching (see Figure 8.1). This technique permits fibre sharing and laser sharing (in the local exchange) for several customers. A TDM signal is broadcast from the exchange to all terminals on a single optical wavelength.

After detection by an optical receiver, each customer's equipment demultiplexes only the channels intended for that destination.

In the return direction, data from the customers is inserted at a predetermined time to arrive at the exchange within an allocated time-slot.

This simple PON architecture admittedly has some drawbacks, e.g.:

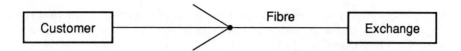

Figure 8.1: *Passive optical network technology*

- Limited bandwidth for interactive services per customer

- Multiplexing of upstream signals requires sophisticated measures

- Privacy and security problems may arise

- Restricted upgradability (how to overcome this problem will be discussed later on).

The PON concept can well support:

- unidirectional distribution services (TV and sound programmes)

- telephony and other 64 kbit/s ISDN services.

Different optical wavelengths $\lambda_1, \ldots, \lambda_n$ may be employed to separate services (and, possibly, transmission directions), e.g. λ_1 for telephony, λ_2 for broadcast TV, λ_3 for video retrieval services etc; see Figure 8.2. Note that different customers may wish to receive different service mixes.

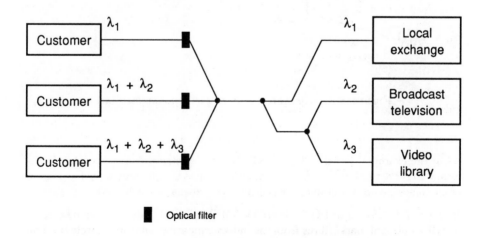

Figure 8.2: *Upgraded passive optical network*

In the long term it might be feasible according to [92] to provide a separate wavelength to every customer with a specific mix of services multiplexed on to the wavelength as required by the customer. However, this concept can only work as long as the number of customers connected to one PON is not too large.

Several modifications of the above concept are conceivable. Instead of wavelength division multiplexing (WDM) (i.e. use of several λ_i) or in addition to WDM, more than one fibre could be installed, e.g. one for TV distribution and the other for interactive services. Implementation of both service categories could thus be decoupled to a great extent.

Figure 8.3 shows an access configuration where two fibres are deployed, one for TV distribution and the other for telephony (or 64 kbit/s ISDN services). After conversion of optical signals into electrical ones close to the customers' premises, a bus-structured coaxial distribution system is used to deliver TV programmes to the customers, and a star structure is used to provide a customer with a copper-based two-wire telephony access.

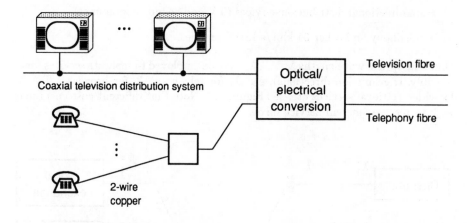

Figure 8.3: *Alternative fibre to the home architecture*

As in the example shown in Figure 8.3 the opto-electrical conversion that is necessary to serve present electrical terminal interfaces is done only once for a couple of customers, so considerable economizing on cost may be achieved.

In view of developing a PON towards a full B-ISDN, it may be advantageous to install additional 'dark' fibres from the outset which are not immediately used but can support later point-to-point connections of individual customers to the local exchange (cf. [123]).

8.2 Introduction of B-ISDN Services

Deployment of optical fibre in the customer access network need not automatically be combined with the introduction of B-ISDN services in the network as has been pointed out in the previous section. Although B-ISDN is conceived to support – at least in the long run – all types of services, the customers' main interest in the new B-ISDN will be concentrated on services that cannot be offered (or only at greater expense) by existing networks.

B-ISDN will therefore co-exist in the beginning with other networks like public data networks, analog telephone networks, 64 kbit/s ISDN, TV distribution networks etc. The services offered by B-ISDN might be restricted to 'typical' broadband services, e.g. interactive services with bit rates above 1.5 Mbit/s or 2 Mbit/s, respectively. Access to other services (e.g. 64 kbit/s ISDN bearer services) would still be provided by other existing interfaces like that according to CCITT Recommendation I.430 (basic access) [60].

Interworking facilities between B-ISDN and the other networks would have to be provided as, for example, a customer using a bifunctional video-telephony/telephony set should be able to communicate with 64 kbit/s ISDN telephony users. This quite simple B-ISDN overlay model is shown in Figure 8.4.

Another step might be to introduce integrated access to different networks via a single, optical fibre-based B-ISDN interface on the network side of the B-NT1.

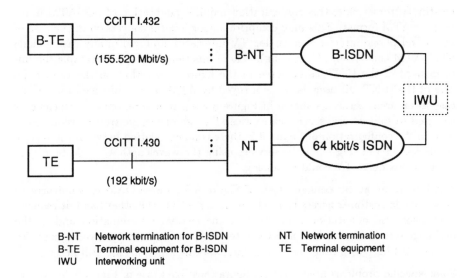

B-NT	Network termination for B-ISDN	NT	Network termination
B-TE	Terminal equipment for B-ISDN	TE	Terminal equipment
IWU	Interworking unit		

Figure 8.4: *Pure B-ISDN overlay network*

This configuration is depicted in Figure 8.5.

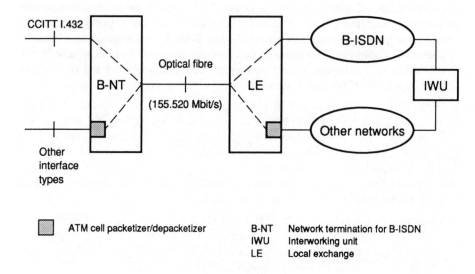

Figure 8.5: *Integrated access configuration*

On the customer side, this configuration requires adaptation of non-ATM interfaces to ATM format. This may comprise analog/digital conversion in the case of analog telephone interfaces or analog TV interfaces, and will in any case include STM/ATM conversion (ATM-izing). These functions could, for example, be implemented in the B-NT as depicted in the figure. Note that on the right-hand side of the B-NT, all user data is conveyed by ATM cells. This need not be the case in an architecture as shown in Figure 8.2 where several optical wavelengths are used to split several service categories. Though one single transmission link is used in the configuration of Figure 8.2, there is no correlation between the service categories offered. For example, services using the wavelength λ_1 could be digital whereas broadcast TV could be analog.

The integrated access configuration of Figure 8.5 reduces OAM expenditures as only a single customer access has to be maintained. On the other hand, it requires conversion and adaptation equipment at the customer termination and at the exchange termination as long as STM interfaces, terminals and networks exist. To connect B-ISDN with other networks, interworking functions are still necessary.

Some specific problems arise with configurations like those of Figure 8.5. As signals from different networks may be multiplexed on one single access line, OAM activities on this access line have to be performed in a way that will not interfere with connections actually established by any network. Therefore, an entity responsible for coordination of OAM activities on a customer's access is required.

The ATM-izing of non-ATM signals in the B-NT and in the corresponding unit in the network can be effected in different ways. Considering, for example, the basic access signal which comprises two 64 kbit/s B channels, the 16 kbit/s D signalling channel and transmission and OAM overhead, either the entire signal could be ATM-ized or each channel separately. In the latter case the mapping of the 16 kbit/s signalling D channel on signalling VC/VP connections would also have to be defined. Information contained in the overhead of the basic access signal need not be transmitted completely to the network, e.g. the framing bits of CCITT Recommendation I.430 [60] are no longer required. However, OAM information like activation/deactivation indication may still have to be exchanged between the B-NT and the network.

The choice of the mapping of the 64 kbit/s ISDN basic access signal on the cell stream of the ATM-based B-ISDN interface may depend on the signal processing in the network. When 64 kbit/s ISDN connections and B-ISDN connections are routed to separate switches – the former to a STM switch, the latter to an ATM switch – then it is advantageous to have a compact basic access signal including its relevant signalling information on a single VC/VP connection. When, however, a common ATM-based B-ISDN switch handles all incoming connections, and separation of 64 kbit/s ISDN connections and broadband connections takes place only behind the local exchange (i.e. into separate trunk networks), use of individual VCCs for the B channels and the D channel information seems to be more adequate.

8.3   Integration of TV Distribution

TV programmes could be offered to the B-ISDN customer as switched or non-switched services (see Figure 8.6).

Figure 8.6(a) shows full integration of TV distribution into B-ISDN. TV programmes are fed into the local exchange which has sole responsibility for operation, administration and maintenance of the customer's access link. Programme selection is done via the usual B-ISDN signalling channels and procedures.

This solution fully complies with the idea of an integrated broadband network; however, it may have market drawbacks. Compared with today's TV distribution to the customer via satellite or cable-based transmission systems, switched TV programmes via optical fibres cannot compete in terms of cost. This fact may inhibit such a solution at least in several countries. Moreover, as the network provider has knowledge about the actual choice of TV programmes to be watched by customers, some critics are concerned about possible infringement upon privacy effected by unauthorized transfer of such knowledge to people who might be

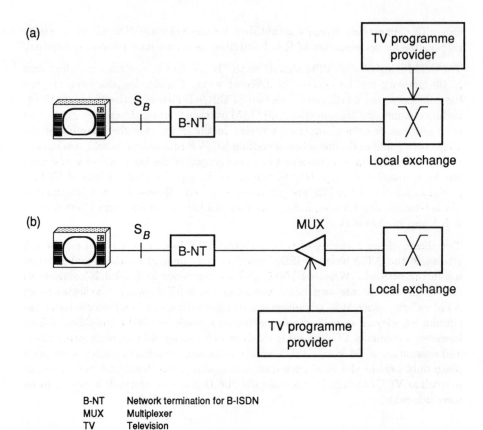

Figure 8.6: *Examples of provision of TV programmes to the B-ISDN customer*

interested in making use of it. From a purely technical viewpoint the provision of switched TV programmes has the highest flexibility as there is in principle no limitation on the number of programmes to be offered.

Figure 8.6(b) shows an architecture where a fixed block of TV programmes is fed from the TV programme provider directly into the access link. The customer can choose a specific programme either in his or her TV set or, optionally, in a customer-owned TV switch (to be located in the B-NT2).

This method limits the number of different TV programmes that can be received due to the limited bandwidth of the access line. The bit rate required for transmission of digital TV signals (including one or more sound channels and additional data channels for control purposes) will be at least about 10 - 30 Mbit/s for conventional TV quality [89] and may be considerably higher for advanced quality pictures. So even with 600 Mbit/s links, only up to about 25 different TV programmes could be transmitted. In the case of future provision of HDTV (high definition TV) which may require 100 Mbit/s or more per TV channel, such a rigid distribution scheme would fail unless more powerful methods like coherent transmission could be employed (cf. Section 10.4).

A mixture of switched and non-switched provision of TV programme channels might also be realized: in addition to a block of some fixed TV channels the user could be given the option to select from a TV programme pool.

TV programme selection (unless merely performed in the customer network) makes some requirements of the signalling procedures. The network must be able to handle quickly numerous simultaneous signalling messages. Changing the TV channel must not take longer than the time that people are used to nowadays. Perhaps this is easier to achieve by (in-band) end-to-end-signalling between user and TV programme provider after establishment of the connection. In this case, however, coordination between the customer equipment (TV sets and/or B-NT2), the local exchange and the TV programme providing unit is necessary to avoid conflicts and to make economic use of the available access line bandwidth. (When, for example, on the customer's premises a TV set is switched on and a TV channel is selected, a new connection normally has to be established unless the required TV channel is already provided to another TV set. If a new connection is to be established, it must be checked in the network, e.g. in the local exchange, whether this can be done without interference with other currently existing connections on the customer's access line.)

8.4 Integration of LANs/MANs into B-ISDN

8.4.1 Local Area Networks

Local area networks (LANs) are primarily employed for data communications in the in-house area. They are used for the interconnection of terminals, workstations, hosts, printers, databases as well as manufacturing systems. The traffic carried is characterized by short data bursts requiring high transmission speed. Normally, only connectionless services are supported by LANs.

LANs cover an area of up to 10 km. One hundred or more users can share a common transmission medium with a transmission speed in the range of usually 1 - 16 Mbit/s. The access to the common medium is controlled by the *media access control* (MAC) procedure (decentralized control).

The number and types of LANs have dramatically increased within the last few years. LANs can be classified by their topology (bus, ring, star), the transmission medium (twisted pair, coax cable, optical fibre) or the MAC procedure (carrier sense multiple access, token passing). In the following, only the most frequently deployed LAN types will be presented. These LANs have different MAC protocols whereas in higher layers identical protocols may be used.

The *carrier sense multiple access with collision detection* (CSMA/CD) is the first standardized MAC procedure [110]. It is based on a development by Xerox called *Ethernet*. CSMA/CD uses a bus system with a specified transmission rate of 10 Mbit/s. A station having a packet to send listens to the carrier before sending. If the channel is idle the station begins sending, otherwise it waits till the channel becomes idle. Collision may occur when two or more stations begin sending at the same time. This will be detected by the sending stations and they will stop their packet transmission. The collision is resolved by the back-off algorithm (each station tries to send after a random time). In low loaded systems, this protocol behaves very well (low packet delay). But due to collisions the performance deteriorates with increasing load.

The *token bus* system [111] uses a coax cable with specified transmission rates of 1, 5 or 10 Mbit/s. All stations are passively coupled to the medium. Access to the channel is controlled by a token-passing protocol. The token is delivered from one station to its neighbour. The neighbourhood is not related to physical locations but defined by addresses. The number of packets which can be sent during the interval a station possesses the token is determined by the token-passing protocol. In order to fulfil different performance requirements, each station uses four internal priority classes.

The *token ring* network [112] is made up of point-to-point unidirectional links interconnecting adjacent stations (active coupling) in order to form a closed loop. Transmission rates of 4 and 16 Mbit/s are specified for shielded twisted pair cables. The access to the ring is again controlled by a token-passing protocol. A station that is ready to send a packet has to wait for the token, which it will receive from its physical neighbour. Different priorities can be attached to tokens but only one token can circulate at a time. During high load situations, token protocols prevent packet collisions whereas for low network load their performance is not very good due to the token rotation time.

8.4.2   Metropolitan Area Networks

The increasing demand for data communication beyond the local area leads to the introduction of *metropolitan area networks* (MANs). MANs can be considered as an evolution of LANs, and their first application will be the interconnection of existing LANs. The characteristic features of MANs are [16, 147]:

- Covering areas of more than 50 km in diameter
- Sharing a common medium
- Distributed access control

- High transmission rate (100 Mbit/s or more)
- Provision of isochronous, connection-oriented and connectionless services
- Evolution to B-ISDN in terms of capabilities and services.

The expected MAN installations can be divided into the *private* and *public* MAN [124]. A private MAN will be owned or leased by a single customer. Only that customer's traffic is carried by the MAN. This simplifies billing as well as functions of privacy and security.

However, many MANs will be shared by a varying number of customers. From the point of view of the network operator, functions for accurate billing and additional management functions are necessary. Security and privacy will become serious issues because customers would not like to see their confidential data passing through the building of their competitor.

8.4.2.1   Fibre-Distributed Data Interface II

The fibre-distributed data interface II (FDDI-II) [5] could be used for MAN implementation. This is an enhanced version of FDDI [113] which is a ring system using an optical fibre for transmission with a data rate of 100 Mbit/s. The access to the ring is controlled by a modified token-passing protocol which is specially designed for high speed transmission systems.

For reasons of reliability, two rings (with opposite transmission directions) are used which make the system capable of surviving a cable break or station failure. In the case of such a failure, only one ring will be used. The total length of both rings is limited to 200 km. Up to 1000 stations with a maximum distance between two stations of 2 km can be attached to the ring.

FDDI supports only packet-switched traffic types. In addition to these traffics, FDDI-II is able to handle isochronous traffic like voice or video.

8.4.2.2   Distributed Queue Dual Bus

The *distributed queue dual bus* (DQDB) which has been proposed as a MAN/LAN standard [108] is the result of the continued development of the *queue packet and synchronous circuit exchange* (QPSX) [126]. Isochronous, connection-oriented and connectionless services can be supported simultaneously.

The DQDB MAN consists of two unidirectional buses with opposite transmission directions and a multiplicity of nodes attached to these buses (see Figure 8.7). DQDB is independent of the underlying physical medium. This allows the use of existing PDH systems with transmission rates of, for example, 34, 45 and 140 Mbit/s [32] as well as SDH-based transmission systems according to [34, 35, 36] and possibly future systems with transmission rates in the Gbit/s range.

Bus A

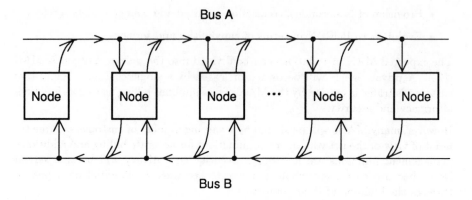

Bus B

Figure 8.7: *Distributed queue dual bus network*

The dual buses can be looped or open ended. In the looped bus the head and tail of each bus are co-located but not interconnected. Looping allows the reconfiguration of the bus system in the case of bus failures. Head and tail will then be interconnected, and close to the location of the failure, new head and tail points will be generated. Each node can act as head or tail. Due to this self-healing mechanism the looped bus configuration seems preferable.

All information in the DQDB network is transported within *slots*. A slot consists of a header with 5 octets and an information field with 48 octets. Its size is identical to the size of an ATM cell. In Appendix B the PDUs used for connectionless services in the B-ISDN are compared with those used in the DQDB network. The commonality of DQDB and B-ISDN simplifies the interconnection of these two networks.

At the head of each bus the slot generator is located. It creates empty slots and writes them on the bus. Isochronous services use *pre-arbitrated* slots. These slots are marked by the slot generator and have the appropriate VCI value inserted in the slot header.

All non-isochronous information is transported within *queue-arbitrated* slots. Pre-arbitrated and queue-arbitrated slots are distinguished by different values in the *slot type* field of the slot header. The queue-arbitrated slots are managed by the distributed queueing protocol (media access control). In contrast to the existing MAC procedures in a distributed queue system, each station buffers the actual number of slots waiting for access in the total network. With this in mind, a station which has a slot ready to send determines its own position in the distributed queue. After satisfying the queued slots its own slot will be transported.

8.4.3 Interworking Units

For many years the need for interconnection of individual computing systems and terminals has been increasing. Today, numerous networks co-exist and the increasing communication requirements demand the interconnection of these networks. For this purpose, *interworking units* (IWUs) are necessary.

Two networks which are located close to each other can be coupled directly via an IWU. Networks which are far from each other can only be interconnected via intermediate subnetworks.

For the following description it is assumed that different protocols are used at layer $(N - 1)$. The protocols of layer N and above are identical in the networks which will be interconnected. Coupling of networks can be achieved by different approaches [15, 139]:

1. Interconnection of the heterogeneous systems is achieved by protocol conversion on layer $(N - 1)$. Often, this protocol transformation is difficult and not all functionalities can be maintained after the conversion because functions in one network are not present in the other one.

2. In the second approach, a common global protocol sublayer is placed on top of the different network protocols. This requires an additional adaptation sublayer between all layer $(N - 1)$ protocols and the common global protocol.

3. Coupling of two networks can also be performed at the first common layer. This approach avoids difficult protocol conversion but it results in higher transfer delay due to the processing of an additional layer within the IWU.

Beyond the selection of a protocol level at which different networks will be interconnected the IWU is also involved in other important issues. *Naming, addressing* and *routing* are the functions which are necessary for the correct delivery of data to its appropriate destination. *Congestion control* has to be applied if the speeds of the networks mismatch. When different maximum packet sizes are defined for the individual networks the IWU has to perform *segmentation* and *reassembly* functions.

For today's networks the following interconnection approaches are commonly used:

- A *repeater* interconnects two networks at layer 1. Its main purpose is the enlargement of small networks.

- Interconnection at layer 2 is performed by *bridges*.

- A *router* interconnects two networks at layer 3.

- An IWU coupling networks at higher layers is called a *gateway*. Normally, only layer 4 gateways and application layer gateways (layer 7) are used.

8.4.4   Integration Scenarios

The first step in coupling LANs was the interconnection via existing networks like the *circuit switched public data network* (CSPDN), the *packet switched public data network* (PSPDN) or the ISDN. LANs use transmission rates of up to 16 Mbit/s whereas in the existing networks the transmission rates are very low (e.g. 64 kbit/s). Obviously, this interworking strategy has no good performance.

In order to achieve good LAN-like services across wide areas, LANs will be coupled via high speed networks like MANs or the B-ISDN. Several evolutionary steps are described below that could follow in chronological order (cf. [22]).

8.4.4.1   Interconnection of LANs via MANs

Nowadays, MANs are becoming a reality [147] whereas B-ISDN is still in the planning and development phase. So in the first evolutionary stage, LANs are coupled via IWUs to MANs. Figure 8.8 shows the present application of MANs.

The MAN may be private or public. In both cases the increasing communication requirements will lead to the interconnection of MANs via dedicated links (see Figure 8.8).

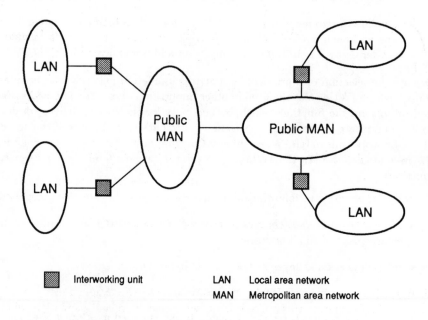

	Interworking unit	LAN	Local area network
		MAN	Metropolitan area network

Figure 8.8: *Interconnection of LANs via MANs*

At first, MANs will only provide connectionless services and be used for LAN interconnection. But in a future stage, MANs could be extended to support isochronous and connection-oriented services.

8.4.4.2   Interconnection of MANs via B-ISDN

The introduction of B-ISDN will be enforced by the need for interconnecting MANs. This approach allows access to wider areas with more flexibility, low delay and high throughput. Figure 8.9 depicts this evolutionary stage.

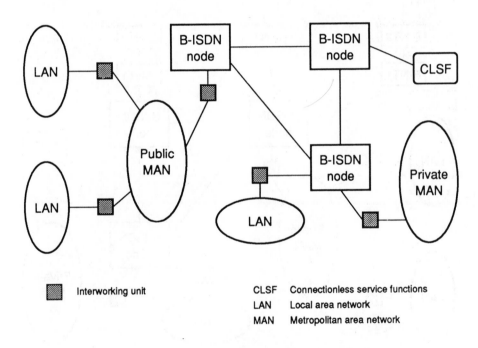

Figure 8.9: *Interconnection of MANs and B-ISDN*

With the introduction of B-ISDN, LANs or private MANs can be directly coupled to the B-ISDN. During this phase it is expected that more and more users will be attracted by the offered services and be encouraged to pass over the initial stage of the evolutionary path and immediately connect to the B-ISDN.

8.4.4.3   Co-existence of MANs and B-ISDN

Simultaneously with the introduction of B-ISDN, broadband terminals and new
broadband CNs will be offered. These new CNs may have a star structure or
they may be shared medium configurations like bus or ring which are well known
from LANs. In Figure 8.10 the intermediate stage is shown when LANs, MANs,
B-ISDN and new CNs co-exist.

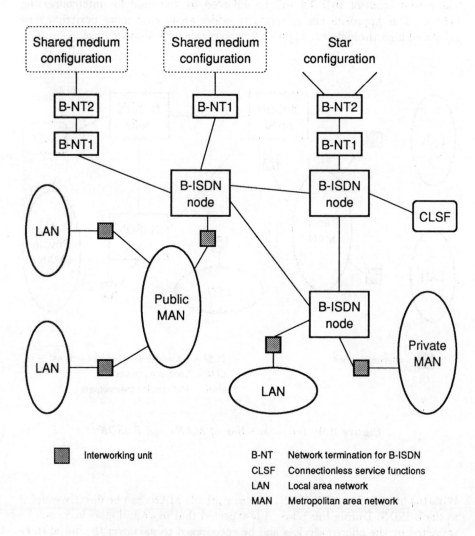

Figure 8.10: *Co-existence of MANs and B-ISDN*

8.4.4.4   Replacement Strategies

It is assumed that B-ISDN is able to offer more flexibility and an equivalent or better set of services with cheaper costs than are available from MANs. Therefore, the spread of MANs will be reduced [94] and in the long term MANs may be pushed out without deterioration of the offered services. Replacement of MANs will start in the trunk network and may end in the local network. The use of MANs in the local network is shown in Figure 7.7. Customers wanting private MANs may also use the B-ISDN as within B-ISDN virtual private networks can be created.

Replacement is not restricted to the public network. It may also happen in the private area. Existing LANs may be substituted by new CNs. These CNs will be based on ATM technology and, in addition to the services supported by LANs, new services with higher bandwidth requirements will be provided.

Figure 8.11 shows the final solution for B-ISDN including CNs with all parts of the network making use of ATM technology.

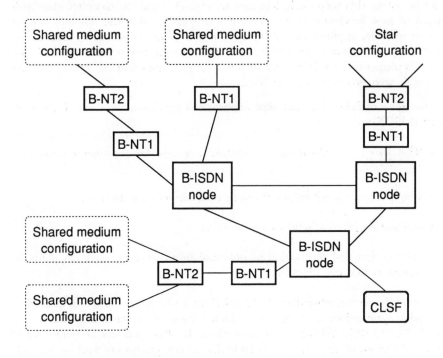

B-NT   Network termination for B-ISDN   CLSF   Connectionless service functions

Figure 8.11: *An overall network based on ATM*

Due to the use of a uniform technique in the whole system, interworking can be kept at low levels. Processing at such low levels will be cheaper and quicker. The user will benefit from better services and lower costs.

8.5   B-ISDN Trials

Many of today's communication requirements can be satisfied by the 64 kbit/s ISDN. However, a few genuine broadband applications already exist. In the in-house area, high speed data communication has been facilitated by LANs, and in the public area, videoconferencing was introduced by using dedicated broadband circuit-switched networks.

Future communication will be characterized by high bandwidth utilization, multi-media applications and point-to-point as well as multipoint connections. These facts require a new network with more intelligence, bandwidth and flexibility. In order to obtain this target solution, new technologies and the complete standardization of new services and interfaces are necessary. But the obvious interest for new services, applications and systems is always accompanied by elements of uncertainty (acceptance, demand, technology, economy and organization). Laboratory implementations, field trials with pilot applications and test networks make it possible to overcome these uncertainties at an early stage.

Further goals of field trials and pilot applications for the preparation of the intelligent B-ISDN are [8]:

- The design of realistic communication scenarios for supporting important applications

- Requirements specification of commercial services and terminals

- Influencing international standardization

- Information and motivation of potential users, service providers, network operators and manufacturers.

All around the world, laboratory ATM switching nodes are realized and field trials with pilot applications and test networks are running or are being planned [8, 12, 82, 83, 98, 136]. Within the framework of the *Research and Development of Advanced Communication in Europe* (RACE), several groups are working towards ATM demonstrators (e.g. the B-ISDN UNI group [18]). Another project – RACE 1012 *Broadband Local Network Technology* (BLNT) – deals with the definition of a second generation ATM-based switching architecture and the development of an experimental switch model [96].

8.5.1 The BERKOM Trial

In 1986 the BERKOM (*Ber*liner *Kom*munikationssystem) project started in Berlin. The objective of this trial is the design, development and demonstration of applications for B-ISDN. The following items are included in the BERKOM project [130]:

- Text and document processing in an office environment
- High quality printing and publishing
- High speed transfer of medical images (e.g. X-ray images)
- Applications in the field of computer-aided design (CAD) and computer-integrated manufacturing (CIM)
- Distribution of high definition television (HDTV) programmes
- Access to information bases containing text, pictures and movies
- Use of high quality audio and video information in the residential area.

In autumn 1989, Siemens installed an ATM switch as part of the BERKOM trial [98]. The switch fabric transfers cells (2 octet header and 30 octet information field) of 16 inlets to 16 outlets, all operating at 140 Mbit/s. The participants are located in Berlin and are attached via single-mode fibres to the ATM switching node.

Typical applications using this ATM switch are (see also Figure 8.12):

- Interconnection of LANs
- Video communications with 64 kbit/s, 2 Mbit/s and 34 Mbit/s
- Joint editing over broadband links
- Interconnection of HICOM-PBXs via ATM (private networking)
- Access to 64 kbit/s ISDN via an EWSD exchange.

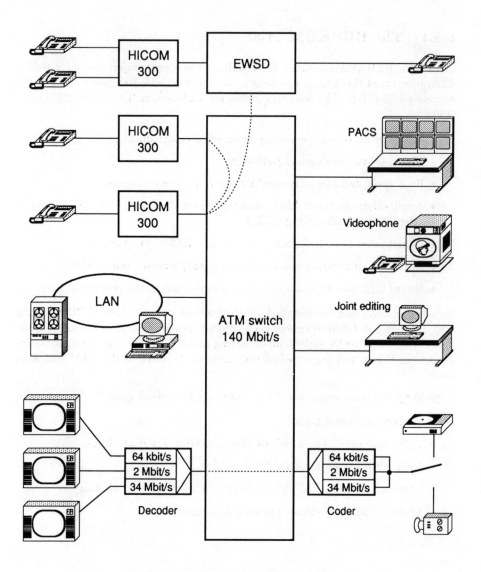

ATM	Asynchronous transfer mode
EWSD	Elektronisches Wählvermittlungssystem Digital
HICOM	High technology communication
LAN	Local area network
PACS	Picture archiving and communication system

Figure 8.12: *ATM applications of the BERKOM trial*

Chapter 9

Miscellaneous

9.1 Connectionless Service in B-ISDN

Besides *connection-oriented* (CO) communication B-ISDN also supports *connectionless* (CL) communication. The provision of CL services in the B-ISDN may be important because one of the first applications in B-ISDN will be the interconnection of LANs/MANs which at present predominantly use CL protocols. As at the B-ISDN ATM layer, only the CO technique exists, so the CL services have to be realized on top of ATM. CCITT Recommendation I.211 [49] describes two mechanisms for supporting CL services in the B-ISDN. In CCITT Recommendation I.327 [53] the concept of CL capabilities within the B-ISDN functional architecture is specified.

9.1.1 Connection-Oriented and Connectionless Communication

A lot of applications like constant bit rate services or X.25 data service [78] are best handled by CO communications. Before the information transfer can start, a connection has to be established. This can be either a physical or a virtual connection. For the connection establishment, a separate procedure is necessary. During this phase the path for the succeeding information transfer will be determined and the necessary resources will be reserved.

However, there exist applications like mail services or other data services which are characterized by sporadic behaviour and a small amount of data. By reason of time and expense, no connection will be established. The user information will be delivered in a message including all necessary addressing and routing information. Each message is handled separately and therefore message sequence integrity cannot be guaranteed. There is also no guarantee of delivery and no acknowledgement of delivery.

171

9.1.2   Indirect Provision of Connectionless Service

In the first approach the CL service is provided indirectly via the B-ISDN CO
service (see Figure 9.1). Between the B-ISDN interfaces, transparent ATM layer
connections are used. These connections may be either permanent, reserved or
on demand. The CL protocols are transparent for the B-ISDN because all CL
services and AAL functions are implemented outside the B-ISDN. CL services are
independent of the protocols within B-ISDN. The support of CL services based on
this approach is always possible.

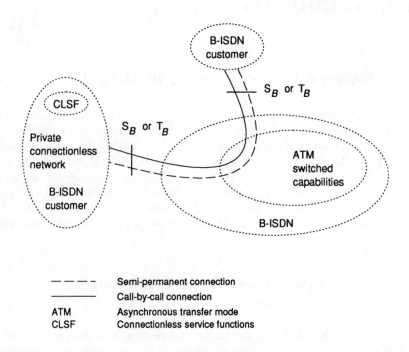

Figure 9.1: *Indirect provision of connectionless service*

The full intermeshing of the B-ISDN interfaces requires a lot of ATM layer connections. The use of permanent and reserved connections results in an inefficient
deployment of these connections whereas switched connections (establishment at
the commencement of the CL service session) lead to an increased signalling traffic
for call/connection control and long call/connection set-up times. One of the characteristic features of the CL services used in LANs or MANs is the short transfer
delay. In order to retain this feature the connection set-up time should also be
very short in B-ISDN.

The indirect provision of CL services is only applicable in the case of a few users of CL services which are attached to B-ISDN. This approach can be considered as an interim solution.

9.1.3 Direct Provision of Connectionless Service

The second approach supports directly the CL service via the B-ISDN (see Figure 9.2). The connectionless service functions (CLSFs) may be located within or outside the B-ISDN and they terminate the CL protocols and route cells to their destination according to the routing information included in the cells.

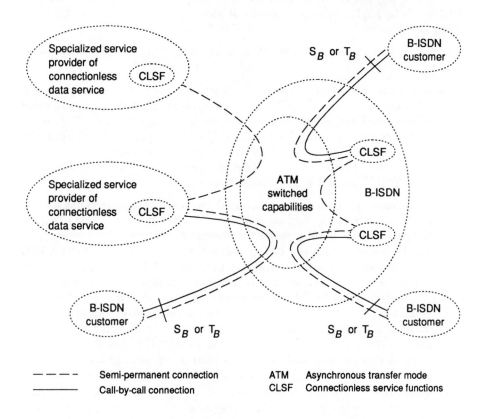

Figure 9.2: *Direct provision of connectionless service*

The CL service is again on top of ATM. This fact requires a connection between each user and the CLSFs which are implemented in the CL server. Such a connection can be either pre-configured, semi-permanent or switched. Semi-permanent connections can be VPCs or VCCs whereas switched connections can only be realized by VCCs. In the case of semi-permanent VPCs, all VCCs within the VPC could be used by CL services.

In the case of switched connections it may occur that a message cannot be delivered from the destination CLSF to the destination user because no connection exists. Then the destination CLSF will reject the message.

The indirect provision of CL services for n users requires $n \times (n - 1)/2$ connections for full intermeshing. In a system with direct provision of CL services and one CL server only, n connections are required for n users. The number of CL servers depends on the size of the B-ISDN and the volume of CL traffic to be handled. CLSFs can be implemented in a specific service node or in a separate part of an ATM switching node.

Two different methods for the handling of CL services in the CL server can be applied:

- In the first case the CL server collects all SAR-PDUs belonging to one CS-PDU and reconstructs this PDU (see Section 5.5). Then the routing function is performed and afterwards the message is segmented again. Due to the reassembly function, this approach requires a high amount of buffer capacity within each CL server. This may cause high transfer delays. The advantage of this method is the feasibility of detecting errored CS-PDUs and discarding those PDUs (unburden the network from worthless PDUs).

- The second approach takes advantage of the fact that after receiving a BOM in the CL server the routing function can already be performed because the payload of a BOM includes the destination address. The routing table will be updated with the correspondence of the incoming VPI/VCI/MID combination and the appropriate outgoing one. All COMs and the EOM belonging to a message are routed by a simple look-up in the routing table. After processing the EOM the corresponding registration in the routing table is deleted. When using this method, only a small buffer capacity per CL message is necessary in each CL server and the transfer delay of a message can be kept low. This approach is similar to the CO technique of the ATM layer. A BOM is processed like a connection set-up message and the routing of the COMs and EOMs can be performed by the same mechanism used for cells.

9.2   Voice Delay and Echo Problems

In an ATM telephone connection, speech samples are collected until they fill the information field of an ATM cell. As the information field consists of 48 octets, a delay of 48/8 kHz = 6 ms is encountered for 64 kbit/s telephony due to the packetization of speech. (If AAL type 1 – cf. Section 5.5.1 – is used for telephony, this delay can be slightly reduced to $47/8$ kHz $= 5.875$ ms; as this is only a small effect it will be neglected in the following consideration.) Depacketization of ATM speech also causes some delay: as individual ATM cells undergo different transfer delays on their way through the network, this delay variation has to be smoothed out at the receiving side in order to generate a constant input required by the speech decoder. This procedure leads to an additional delay of approximately 1 ms.

The resulting total delay may exceed the tolerable limit, especially when there are several transitions from STM to ATM and vice versa within one connection (e.g. in the case of traversing three ATM islands the resulting additional transfer delay due to packetization and depacketization would be $3 \times [6$ ms $+ 1$ ms$] = 21$ ms).

The main problem is not the one-way delay itself but the delayed speaker echo received at the sending side, arising primarily at the far end of the transmission line, specifically at the hybrid junction between four-wire and two-wire analog circuits. The maximum one-way delay permissible for telephone connections is 400 ms according to CCITT Recommendation G.114 [28]. This value has been chosen to take into account connections involving satellite links; for other connections a considerably lower one-way delay can be achieved, as is the case for ATM links.

However, echo received at the sending side will be perceived as disturbing by the speaker at a rather low value for the round-trip delay. As a rule of thumb, echo cancellation should be employed whenever a one-way delay of about 25 ms is exceeded.

Figure 9.3 (based on [28]) gives more information on the echo problem related to ATM speech connections. It is assumed that one ATM area is inserted into an existing analog or digital telephone network. This insertion causes additional delay and therefore aggravates the echo problem. The employment of ATM reduces the transmission length that can be covered without echo control measures. The curves drawn in Figure 9.3 directly show the effect of (non-processed) echo delay on the perception of human beings in terms of 'probability of encountering objectionable echo' (e.g. 1% means that 1% of the speakers complain about the quality of their telephone connection). According to CCITT Recommendation G.131 [29] no more than 1% objections to speech quality should be made in a network, but values up to 10% may be tolerated in exceptional cases.

The 1% limit of objections would confine the transmission length to about 300 km in the case of insertion of one ATM area into an analog environment and to about 650 km in the case of insertion of one ATM area into a digital environment unless echo control was performed.

In Figure 9.3 the loss of the echo path was assumed to be 28 dB. The two isolated spots in the figure have been calculated for local connections (transmission length up to about 50 km) and inter-local connections (transmission length of

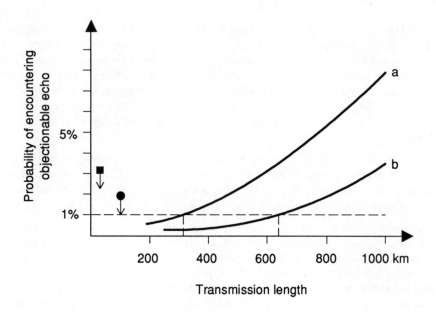

Figure 9.3: *Echo tolerance curves of telephone connections*

about 100 km) with specified losses of 21 dB and 24 dB, respectively, according to (current) US standards (cf. [115]). As the low loss requirements in these cases may be reduced in future, the potential echo problems are expected to decrease; this is indicated in the figure by down-arrows.

To sum it up:

- ATM introduces additional delay and thus increases echo problems in conjunction with speech connections.

- The number of ATM/STM conversions should be kept to a minimum.

- Compared with today's telephone networks, more echo cancellation devices will have to be deployed with ATM. This could however be avoided, if necessary, with partly filled cells in many cases; for example, by filling only 24 octets of the 48 octet cell information field the packetization delay will be halved. The wastage of bandwidth may be tolerable at least in the introductory stage of ATM networks.

9.3 Tariffing in B-ISDN

Tariffing of services in future ATM networks is a crucial factor that will strongly influence the acceptance of B-ISDN by customers.

The following questions may be raised relating to tariffing:

- How can tariffs for ATM networks be made cost-adequate? What tariff components should be defined, and what parameters have to be measured for charging?

- How can a smooth transition from tariffing of services in existing networks to future ATM tariffs be achieved?

First, a brief overview of tariffing in existing networks will be made before we address our topic of how to charge ATM services.

9.3.1 Tariffing in Existing Networks

Two different categories of charges are presently used:

- *Basic rate* (e.g. per month) which is charged for the network access irrespective of a customer's actual traffic load.

- *Traffic charges* which are determined by one or more of the following components:
    - charges for establishing/releasing connections
    - charging per connection time
    - charging per volume
    - flat rate.

For instance, in today's telephone networks, calls are usually charged according to their connection time. The tariffs may vary during the day (higher charges at busy hours) and may depend on the distances to be covered. For data packet networks, volume-dependent tariffing may be chosen, i.e. each packet to be delivered is charged. In addition, small charges for establishing and retaining a connection may also be levied.

These two examples show that different networks may require different tariffing schemes in order to comply with the general requirements of cost-adequate charging and user acceptance (the latter often reflects the historical and social situation in a country and may outweigh the former).

9.3.2   Tariffing in ATM Networks

The ATM-based B-ISDN will supply both stream and packet-type applications. Charging in an ATM network therefore is a complex issue to resolve.

Though in an ATM network all information is transmitted in cells, simple (linearly) volume-dependent tariffing as in conventional packet networks may not be accepted. If a per-cell charge was introduced which led to phone call charges comparable to those of today, a broadband stream communication with a bit rate of, for example, 10 Mbit/s would be so expensive that it would hardly be used.

In the following, requirements on ATM charging derived from the above considerations are listed [102]:

- No change in charges for already existing mass services like telephony, facsimile and data transmission

- Service-independent charging

- Flexibility with respect to the introduction of new services

- Transparency of tariffs

- Due consideration of peak bit rates (as these strongly impact on network dimensioning and costs)

- Fair charging for variable bit rate services

- Keep administrative efforts as low as possible (e.g. avoid cell counting for telephone connections).

A proposal was made in [102] that tries to take into account all these requirements on ATM charging. It is based on:

- a basic rate
- traffic-dependent charges comprising two components:
  - charging for call establishment
  - charging according to duration and bit rate of a call.

The basic rate reflects the cost for provision of the customer access. When a customer wishes to permanently restrict the use of access to a bit rate below the possible maximum bit rate (e.g. the customer only wants 30 Mbit/s), and this actually reduces network access costs, the basic rate may be adjusted accordingly.

As the processing effort for setting up a connection is almost independent of the requested bit rate, call establishment may be charged at the same rate in all cases. However, establishment of virtual connections implies reservation of network resources. By raising different charges for call establishment in the case of prioritized, high quality of service or high bit rate connections, users could be prevented from having reserved network resources that would actually not be needed.

The second component of the traffic-dependent charges – charging per call duration and bit rate – takes into account costs for the usage of transmission systems in the network. This charge would normally increase with the bit rate in a non-linear way. The time unit for charging should be sufficiently small to ensure adequate charging for variable bit rate services. The peak bit rate during this short time unit could be used to determine how much a connection would be charged for.

Such a charging mechanism would reflect the network efforts to support ATM connections better than a plain volume-dependent tariff (i.e. charging per cell).

The discussion on charging in ATM networks within CCITT has yielded some general charging principles as outlined before; detailed charging procedures are not yet available. The following ATM-specific items will have to be taken into account:

- Existence of two cell loss priorities (see Section 5.4.2.7)

- Usage parameter control capabilities (see Section 4.5.1.2)

- Actual resource allocation in the network.

Chapter 10

Outlook

In this book, we have focused on B-ISDN and its appropriate techniques which will be the solution for the arising near-term and medium-term broadband communication needs. While MANs and B-ISDN are becoming a reality (field trials have already been started) people in research laboratories are already reflecting on the next stage. So the ATM-based B-ISDN – like any new concept – faces a two-fold problem concerning its implementation: it has to be accepted by users and network providers in order to replace existing networks, and its full-scale realization may be jeopardized at some point in time by new, competing network concepts.

Such new ideas (some will be briefly discussed in the following), however, need not necessarily render the ATM-based B-ISDN superfluous; on the contrary, they will most probably be incorporated in the B-ISDN to make it an even more powerful telecommunication tool.

10.1   Universal ATM Network: Realistic Target?

The universal integrated ATM-based broadband network is easy to depict (Figure 10.1), but in reality it will most probably be a bit more complicated as in Figure 10.2 for a certain period of time (cf. [100]).

As the ATM network implementation will not start from scratch but will have to take into account existing network services and customer needs, the transition to the universal ATM-based broadband network will take a long time. Perhaps the approach to the so-called *universal ATM target network* will only occur asymptotically with occasional deviations from the ideal line, or some telecommunication service providers may never be convinced to exclusively use ATM-based B-ISDN. At present, no one can know exactly.

In this book, some special technical problems of ATM-based transmission (e.g. when applied to speech connections or TV distribution) have been addressed.

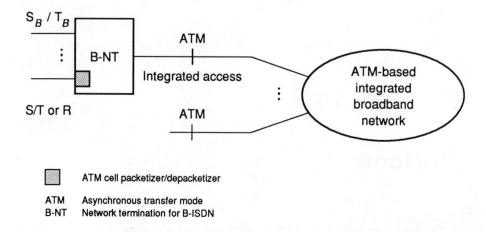

ATM cell packetizer/depacketizer

ATM   Asynchronous transfer mode
B-NT   Network termination for B-ISDN

Figure 10.1: *Universal ATM network*

However, economic facts or acceptance problems may prove more critical than technical items. We want to emphasize that we believe that ATM-based network implementations will become more and more important for the flexible provision of a variety of services, and that the above mentioned observations only apply to the envisaged long-term development towards an all-embracing ATM network. When stepping forward in this direction, even before entering a new evolution stage, its technical impact should be evaluated and careful market and cost analyses should be worked out in order to be able to define the appropriate time scale for the actual ATM network implementation.

In [97] four major areas are mentioned that are decisive – according to the authors' opinion – for the acceptance of ATM. These areas are *quality of service, compatibility, charging* and *scaling*.

Quality of service requirements and their impact on ATM networking have already been discussed in Sections 4.4 and 4.5. It was pointed out there that refined models of the ATM traffic statistics are yet to be developed and possibly sophisticated traffic control and resource management techniques have to be employed to build an efficient ATM network which can meet the quality of service demands of its customers.

Compatibility of ATM with existing or upcoming telecommunication networks: in [97] fear is expressed that existing networks and services may have to sacrifice to the realization of ATM networks; existing networks and services might possibly undergo some changes to cater for the introduction of ATM. An example is the possible need for more echo control devices due to the connection of ATM networks with non-ATM networks (as outlined in Section 9.2). Compatibility be-

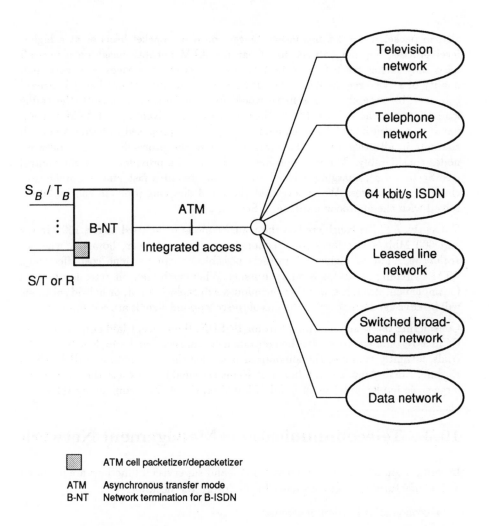

Figure 10.2: *Intermediate state public network architecture*

tween ATM networks and DQDB MANs has been achieved to a certain degree (cf. Section 8.4.2.2). This is deemed an important feature of ATM which facilitates its introduction. Another crucial point is the capability of ATM networks to emulate existing circuit-oriented transmission and to interwork with other networks. Circuit emulation is supported by AAL type 1 (see Section 5.5.1); interworking procedures will be specified in the near future.

One other important feature of ATM networks is *charging* (cf. Section 9.3). Usu-

ally, in packet networks, one either charges on a per-packet basis or at a higher
level process, e.g. per call set-up. Charging ATM network usage on a per-call
basis only makes sense for constant bit rate services or services with very high
quality of service requirements that ask for peak bit rate reservation. (A general
call peak bit rate charging scheme would force customers to smooth the traffic
load offered to the ATM network, thus reducing the advantages of ATM as compared to conventional STM techniques.) In [97] it is proposed to perform per-cell
charging in all other cases. This might increase the processing load in network
nodes considerably. Though counting of cells is to be provided for traffic control
(see Section 4.5), charging per cell additionally requires fast and comprehensive
charging procedures. We believe that the ATM charging problem can be better
solved with the approach outlined in Section 9.3.

Currently, ATM is considered as the transfer mode to be used at the 150 Mbit/s
and 600 Mbit/s interfaces (see Section 5.2). It is not clear, however, whether
scaling of ATM to higher bit rates is possible or can be done cost-effectively.
ATM switching of Gbit/s is an open issue. When such high bit rates are mature
for implementation, maybe other techniques will replace ATM, or hybrid solutions
will be envisaged where only portions of the compound signals are cell-multiplexed.

Considering the available equipment for B-ISDN, the concept laid down in several
CCITT recommendations (to be continuously improved and supplemented), the
trials currently running, the announced plans for the introduction of B-ISDN in
Europe, North America and Japan, it seems reasonable to expect the start of the
large-scale implementation of B-ISDN based on the ATM technique by 1995.

10.2 Telecommunications Management Network

In today's communication systems, control and supervision functions are included
as manufacturer-specific solutions. In the future the need for:

- economic utilization of resources
- flexible allocation of network capacities and features
- installation of virtual private networks

will require a computer-aided telecommunication management system [145]. This
can no longer be a manufacturer-dependent solution. It will be tailored according
to the principles for a telecommunications management network as laid down in
CCITT Recommendation M.30 [66].

The telecommunications management network (TMN) is an independent information processing system. It enables network operators (of public as well as virtual
private networks) to supervise components of the telecommunication network via
defined interfaces and protocols. Figure 10.3 shows the relationship between TMN
and the telecommunication network.

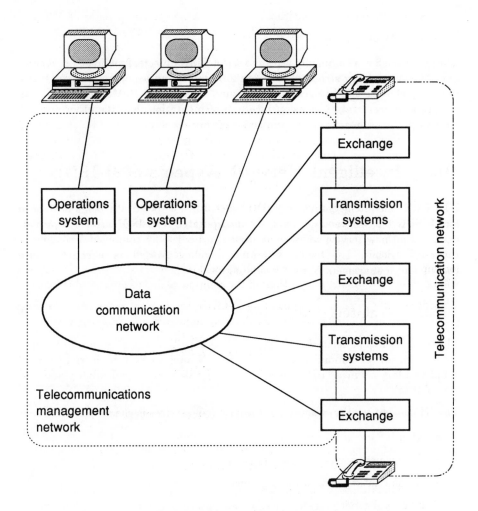

Figure 10.3: *Relationship between telecommunications management network and telecommunication network*

The network management application functions supported by TMN include the following categories [138]:

- Performance management
- Fault management
- Configuration management

- Accounting management

- Security management.

The goal to define a commonly accepted set of TMN objects, functions, procedures and information flow structures is quite ambitious, and a number of experts are presently striving hard to resolve this issue. Nevertheless, TMN seems to be in a more advanced stage in view of future implementation than the other network features to be addressed in the remainder of this chapter.

10.3   Intelligent Network Aspects of B-ISDN

Like TMN, the intelligent network (IN) concept is not specifically being developed for B-ISDN but will most probably be incorporated in B-ISDN. INs will provide existing and new service components that can be flexibly combined according to the user's wishes. INs require powerful signalling procedures, effective service control and management of service-related data.

10.3.1   Architectural Model

The term *intelligent network* is used (according to [26]) 'to describe an architectural concept for all telecommunication networks. IN aims to ease the introduction of supplementary services (UPT, freephone, etc.) based on more flexibility and new capabilities'.

The IN concept for the creation and provision of services is characterized by:

- extensive use of information processing techniques

- efficient use of network resources

- modularization of network functions

- integrated service creation and implementation by means of reusable standard network functions

- flexible allocation of network functions to physical entities

- portability of network functions among physical entities

- standardized communication between network functions via service independent interfaces

- service provider access to the process of composition of services through the combination of network functions

- service subscribers control of subscriber-specific service attributes

- standardized management of service logic.

The functions required for IN and their splitting into functional entities are depicted in Figure 10.4. The main principle is the distribution of service control between call control/service switching and service control. To illustrate this concept, Figure 10.5 gives an example of how these functions are mapped into physical entities of a telecommunication network. Call control/service switching is located in the exchanges. They find out by means of trigger tables whether a call can be completed by themselves or if it has to be handled by the service control point. Interaction between the exchanges and the service control point is effected via the signalling network (e.g. SS7 as shown in Figure 10.5). The special resource functions (located in the example in an intelligent peripheral) may provide, for example, protocol conversion, speech recognition, synthesized speech provision etc.

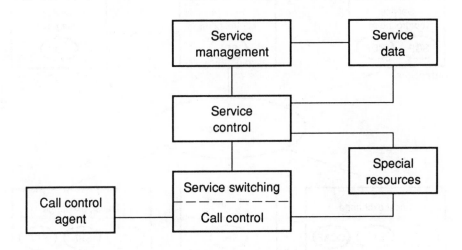

Figure 10.4: *Service execution functional entities*

The service control point contains the IN service logic and handles service-related processing activity. It uses the service data function which provides access to all necessary service-related data and network data and which also performs consistency checks on data.

Finally, the service management function involves service management control, service provision control and service deployment control. Examples of service management control functions are: collection of service statistics, reporting of usage of non-existing freephone numbers, reporting of unauthorized access in a virtual private network. Service provision control handles operation and administration for service provisioning (e.g. creating new subscribers, modifying subscription records). Service deployment control is invoked when introducing a new service

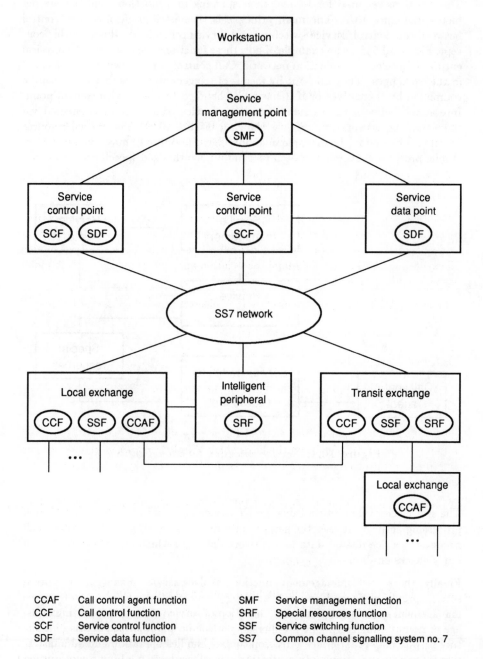

CCAF	Call control agent function	SMF	Service management function
CCF	Call control function	SRF	Special resources function
SCF	Service control function	SSF	Service switching function
SDF	Service data function	SS7	Common channel signalling system no. 7

Figure 10.5: *Example of functions mapping into physical entities*

into the network, and it deals with service logic allocation, signalling and routing definition, service data introduction, allocation of trigger capabilities, special service feature allocation etc.

10.3.2   Overview of IN Services

Following [95] IN services can be grouped into three different categories according to the particular network capabilities that are required for their implementation. Such examples of IN services are described in Table 10.1.

Another broad field of application of IN capabilities is *universal personal telecommunications* (UPT).

[26] describes UPT as follows: 'Universal personal telecommunications is anticipated to bring network personal identification to reality by transparently replacing the static relationship between terminal identity and subscriber identity common in existing networks with a dynamic association and thus provide complete mobility across multiple networks.'

The aim of UPT is to provide user-to-user telecommunication services with:

- network-transparent user identification

- personal mobility

- charging and billing on the basis of the subscriber identity instead of the terminal identity.

The users who have subscribed to the UPT service should be enabled to establish and receive any type of calls on the basis of a network-transparent unique personal telecommunications number (PTN) across multiple networks at any user-network access.

The network capabilities to support UPT can be classified according to [26] into:

- originating network capability

- terminating network capability.

Table 10.2 gives an overview of the main functions required for UPT.

IN services as outlined above will have to be offered by any future public network, including B-ISDN. 'IN and ISDN enhance one another because they provide complementary capabilities with respect to network services, i.e. flexible service control on the one hand and powerful user-network access and network-internal signalling on the other hand' [95].

Category	Service	Description
B (called party) number services	Basic green number service (freephone service)	Toll-free service paid for by called party. Special access code, e.g. 800, serves as trigger.
A + B (calling and called party) number services	Alternate billing service	Allows the user to bill the call to a number other than the A-number.
	Enhanced emergency response service	Dialling of a special countrywide emergency number serves as a trigger. The service control point determines the appropriate emergency response control number for call completion.
	Virtual private network	Provides the functionality of private/dedicated networks using the shared facilities of the public network.
	Area wide CENTREX	Offers dynamic resource allocation and uniform numbering plan over geographically dispersed locations. The CENTREX service utilizes a public network local exchange to provide PBX-like features to a group of business customers. Area wide CENTREX interconnects multiple customer locations as if they were on a single switch.
Interactive services	Interactive green number service	Allows the user to select one of a set of offered alternatives associated with a single green number.
	Voice messaging	Requires a user dialog for entering control commands, for example.
	Call completion	Comprises various features to assist the calling party in completing the call to the called party.

Table 10.1: *Intelligent network services*

Capability	Requested Functions
Originating network capability	UPT service identification
	Routing to home network
	Interrogation
	Connection to routing address
Terminating network capability	Location registration
	PTN paging or announcement
	Paging or announcement response
Home network capability	Authentication of users
	Translation of PTN into routing address
	Location management
	Service management

Table 10.2: *Functions required for UPT*

10.4   Coherent Optical Transmission

Presently used optical transmission systems with bit rates up to some Gbit/s do not make complete use of the bandwidth that is basically provided by light waves (a wavelength of 1500 nm corresponds to a frequency of 200 THz). This is due to the fact that existing systems deploy lasers to emit light and photo-diodes to detect it which can only differentiate between light intensities. So the intensity of the emitted light is the only optical parameter to be modulated in this case which is called *direct* optical transmission.

To enhance the transmission capabilities of optical systems, wavelength division multiplexing (WDM) can be used. Here, several lasers send with different wavelengths. These wavelengths can be modulated independently of each other. They can be combined on to a single optical transmission line by means of an optical star coupler. At the receiving side, the different wavelengths are separated by optical filters. However, this method has the drawback that several lasers are needed; furthermore, currently existing optical filters have a huge bandwidth that impedes fine structuring of the available signal bandwidth.

A much more promising approach is *coherent optical transmission* [116, 143]. It is based upon the superposition of a locally generated, second light wave (of near-by wavelength) with the received wave and detection of the beat (characterized by its relatively slowly oscillating amplitude) by a photo-diode. Coherent transmission makes much higher use of the bandwidth available on optical transmission links due to this frequency shift. Frequencies of the optical spectrum can thus be employed with almost no gaps in between. For coherent transmission, all types of modulation can be used, e.g. amplitude shift keying, frequency shift keying and phase shift keying. Coherent transmission gets close to the physical limits (due to the quantum structure of light) of optical detection; whereas direct optical transmission requires 1700 photons per bit, coherent transmission is reported [93] to get down to a tremendous figure of 9 photons per bit (for transmission of 140 Mbit/s with a bit error ratio of 10^{-9}).

However, coherent optical transmission imposes several problems on its implementation. High accuracy lasers are required; in contrast to direct optical transmission, disturbances of frequency, phase and polarization have to be suppressed as they influence the detected signal. A special problem is that the superposed light waves must have the same polarization but this is not trivial to achieve as the polarization of the light wave changes when propagating through the optical fibre.

Though the flexibility of coherent optical transmission has been demonstrated at several places around the world, the goal to develop mature systems suitable for mass production is still to be reached. Integration of optical components will play an outstanding role.

As a long-term option, coherent optical transmission could, for instance, be used to distribute a large number of high quality television (e.g. HDTV) programmes on a single optical fibre. Even if about 1 Gbit/s per (uncompressed) HDTV channel were consumed, the bit rate provided by coherent optical transmission would be more than sufficient to accommodate hundreds of different channels.

10.5   Gbit/s Local Area Networks

Currently, LANs can satisfy throughput requirements in the 100 Mbit/s range (e.g. FDDI [113]). But there exist other communication requirements, like interconnection of supercomputers with high resolution graphic terminals or the need for a high speed backbone network, which demand networks in the Gbit/s range.

At these high speeds, only optical fibres are suitable for the physical medium. In point-to-point systems, Gbit/s are already used; however, LANs are much more complicated.

Research on LANs in the Gbit/s range has already started. A lot of problems exist which have to be solved in the future. Some of these open questions are:

- Optical power limitation [104]
- Electronic bottleneck [104]
- Network topologies [1]
- Medium access control [125]
- Definition of protocols for high speed applications
- Compatibility with B-ISDN.

Interconnection of such very high speed LANs would obviously require high speed links, e.g. 600 Mbit/s links.

10.6 Optical Switching

In the B-ISDN which is currently under development, optical transmission and electronic switching are used. For most of the services envisaged today, a switched bit rate of 600 Mbit/s seems to be sufficient. Only in the area of holographic imaging are Tbit rates discussed.

In the existing experimental switching systems, CMOS as well as emitter coupled logic techniques are applied which allow the implementation of systems up to the Gbit range. In the future, a speed-up to the range of a few Gbits will be achieved using gallium arsenide. However, this seems to be the limit of electronic switching.

Different reasons for optical switching exist [127]:

Historical perspective: Analog transmission was followed by electro-mechanical switching. Then digital transmission was introduced which was followed by digital switching. Now optical transmission is used, and if history repeats again, optical switching will be the next step.

Speed limitation: As already mentioned above the speed of electronic switching will be limited in the lower Gbit range (approximately 10 Gbit/s). Higher speed requires optical switching.

Cost reduction: In systems with optical transmission and electronic switching, optical/electrical and electrical/optical interfaces are necessary. These expensive units can be avoided by staying entirely in the optical range.

As a first step, optical switching can be introduced in pure space division multiplexing systems using optical switching matrices. User information need nowhere be converted from the optical to the electrical range and vice versa in the individual switching nodes. Control of the switching matrices is only necessary at the set-up and release of a connection. Therefore, this can be performed by electronics.

However, in B-ISDN, asynchronous time division multiplexing is used. Information is transported in cells. This requires some processing of the cell header in each switching element in order to transport the cell to its proper destination output. Cell header processing requires extensive logic manipulations, and if this is done by electronics, optical conversion is necessary and cost reduction will not be very significant. This disadvantage can be avoided by using optical computing and optical memories for cell header processing. In today's ATM systems and in future systems up to the lower Gbit range, cell header processing can still be performed by electronics. However, higher speeds will definitely require optical processing.

Other drawbacks of optical switching like optical losses must be overcome. Furthermore, the inherent regeneration and amplification in digital electronic switching needs some counterpart in optical switching.

And lastly, optical switching will only have success in the competition against electronic switching if it can be implemented economically.

As a conclusion, large-scale implementation of optical switching will not take place very soon and it may need some decades to replace the presently used electronic switching techniques. But optical subsystems (e.g. optical switching matrices for space division multiplexing) may be introduced much more quickly.

Appendix A

B-ISDN Standardization

A.1 Overview

In order that any two customers can indeed communicate with each other via B-ISDN, a variety of standards have to be agreed worldwide. Such standards will be set by certain standards bodies, amongst which the CCITT plays an outstanding role in the context of B-ISDN as it produces international standards (called *recommendations*).

In Table A.1 (see pages 198 and 199) the currently existing B-ISDN related CCITT recommendations are listed and briefly described. The scope of application of these recommendations is illustrated by Figure A.1.

Open issues which will lead to future enhancement of the existing recommendations or to new supplementary recommendations are indicated in the following sections.

A.2 Open Issues

The main open issues to be resolved with respect to the existing B-ISDN recommendations are briefly described in this section.

1. ATM (CCITT Recommendations I.150 and I.361):
   - Detailed description of the use of the payload type field
   - Generic flow control functions, procedures and coding
   - Management functions of the ATM layer (e.g. VPI/VCI assignment, meta-signalling, ATM link maintenance).

2. Network aspects (CCITT Recommendation I.311):
   - Detailed description of traffic control procedures.

3. Protocol reference model (CCITT Recommendation I.321):

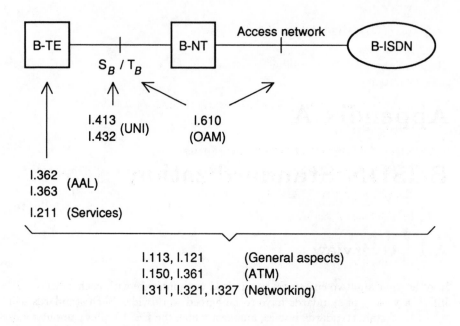

ATM   Asynchronous transfer mode   B-TE   Terminal equipment for B-ISDN
AAL   ATM adaptation layer   OAM   Operation and maintenance
B-NT   Network termination for B-ISDN   UNI   User-network interface

Figure A.1: *Application scope of B-ISDN recommendations*

- Alignment with OSI layered model still pending.

4. User-network interface (CCITT Recommendations I.413 and I.432):
   - Interface at S_B reference point
   - Structure of 622.080 Mbit/s interface
   - Cell-based interface option
   - Modes of interface operation
   - Electrical/optical parameters.

5. Services (CCITT Recommendation I.211):
   - Bit rates of constant/variable bit rate services
   - Service parameter definition
   - Charging.

6. AAL (CCITT Recommendations I.362 and I.363):
   - Completion of AAL type 1-3 SAR field formats and coding
   - Convergence sublayer protocols.

A.3 Supplementary Topics

Supplementary B-ISDN recommendations have to be prepared by CCITT on the following topics:

- B-ISDN service descriptions (e.g. connectionless data service)
- Connection types
- Quality of service and network performance
- Signalling protocols to support B-ISDN (access/internodal signalling)
- General aspects of OAM of the network
- B-ISDN access network
- ATM trunk network
- Interworking specifications
- ATM switch characteristics.

(This list is not exhaustive.)

Number: Title	Contents
I.113: Vocabulary of terms for broadband aspects of ISDN	Definition of terms used for B-ISDN
I.121: Broadband aspects of ISDN	Principles of B-ISDN

I.150:
B-ISDN ATM functional characteristics
	• Functions of the ATM layer (cell header):
	  virtual channel connection
	  virtual path connection
	  payload type
	  cell loss priority
	  generic flow control

I.211: B-ISDN service aspects	• Classification and general description of B-ISDN services • Network aspects of multi-media services • Service timing, synchronization aspects • Connectionless data service aspects • Video-coding aspects

I.311:
B-ISDN general network aspects
	• Networking techniques:
	  virtual channel (VC) level
	  virtual path (VP) level
	  VC and VP links/connections
	• Signalling principles:
	  signalling requirements
	  signalling VCs at the user access
	  meta-signalling channel
	• Traffic control:
	  connection admission control
	  usage parameter control
	  priority control
	  congestion control

I.321: B-ISDN protocol reference model and its application	• Extension of I.320 • Overview of functions in layers and sublayers • Distinction between physical layer and ATM layer functions
I.327: B-ISDN functional architecture	• Enhancement of I.324 • Basic architecture model, network capabilities • Reference connection, connection elements • Connectionless service function, access via VCCs or VPCs
I.361: B-ISDN ATM layer specification	• ATM cell structure 5 octet header + 48 octet information field • Coding of cell header

Table A.1: *List of CCITT recommendations for B-ISDN*

Number: Title	Contents

I.362:
B-ISDN ATM adaptation layer (AAL) functional description
	• Basic principles of the AAL:
	  service dependent
	  may be empty for some applications
	• Sublayering of the AAL:
	  Segmentation and reassembly (SAR) sublayer and
	  convergence sublayer (CS)
	• 4 AAL service classes based on:
	  timing relation source/sink
	  constant/variable bit rate
	  connection-oriented/connectionless mode

I.363:
B-ISDN ATM adaptation layer (AAL) specification
	• 4 AAL protocol types defined with respect to:
	  services
	  SAR/CS functions
	  SAR-PDU structure and coding

I.413: B-ISDN user-network interface	• Reference configurations • Examples of physical configurations • Interfaces at T_B and S_B: 155.520 (622.080) Mbit/s
I.432: B-ISDN user-network interface – physical layer specification	• Electrical/optical parameters • Interface structure (e.g. SDH frame) • Header error control generation/verification • Cell delineation

I.610:
OAM principles of the B-ISDN access
	• OAM principles:
	  hierarchical structure of OAM functions and information flows
	• OAM functions for B-ISDN UNI and access network
	• Implementation of OAM functions of the physical layer for the
	  SDH-based UNI

Table A.1: *List of CCITT recommendations for B-ISDN (continued)*

Appendix B

B-ISDN and DQDB Protocols

B.1   Correlation between B-ISDN and DQDB

Figure B.1 shows the protocol stacks for CL services in B-ISDN and DQDB. The correlations between the two protocol stacks are identified by dashed lines. As long as the CS protocol of the AAL is not completely defined, the exact relationship between the AAL and the DQDB layer cannot be described.

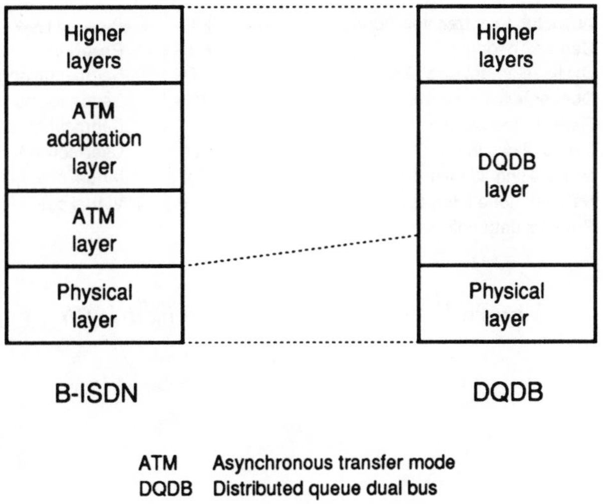

Higher layers		Higher layers
ATM adaptation layer		DQDB layer
ATM layer		
Physical layer		Physical layer
B-ISDN		**DQDB**

ATM   Asynchronous transfer mode
DQDB   Distributed queue dual bus

Figure B.1: *Protocol layering in B-ISDN and DQDB*

201

B.2   CL-PDU Hierarchy in B-ISDN

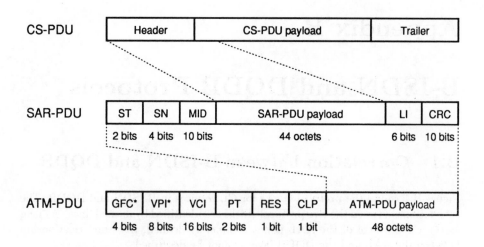

* This ATM-PDU is valid at the B-ISDN UNI. At the B-ISDN NNI the GFC field is not available and
the VPI field is extended to 12 bits.

ATM	Asynchronous transfer mode	PT	Payload type
CLP	Cell loss priority	RES	Reserved
CRC	Cyclic redundancy check	SAR	Segmentation and reassembly
CS	Convergence sublayer	SN	Sequence number
GFC	Generic flow control	ST	Segment type
LI	Length indicator	UNI	User-network interface
MID	Multiplexing identifier	VCI	Virtual channel identifier
NNI	Network-node interface	VPI	Virtual path identifier
PDU	Protocol data unit		

Figure B.2: *CL-PDU hierarchy in B-ISDN*

B.3 CL-PDU Hierarchy in DQDB

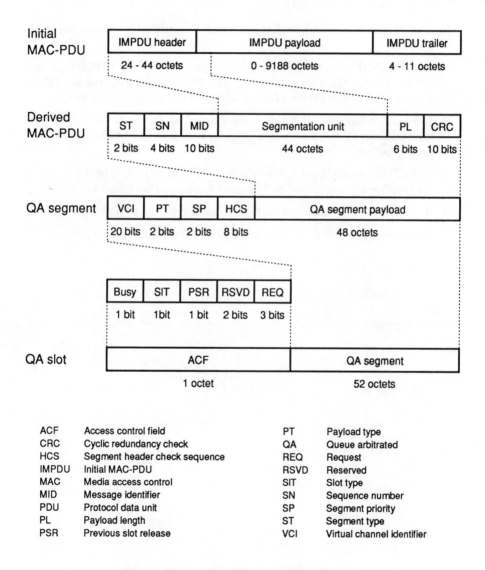

ACF	Access control field		PT	Payload type
CRC	Cyclic redundancy check		QA	Queue arbitrated
HCS	Segment header check sequence		REQ	Request
IMPDU	Initial MAC-PDU		RSVD	Reserved
MAC	Media access control		SIT	Slot type
MID	Message identifier		SN	Sequence number
PDU	Protocol data unit		SP	Segment priority
PL	Payload length		ST	Segment type
PSR	Previous slot release		VCI	Virtual channel identifier

Figure B.3: *CL-PDU hierarchy in DQDB*

B.4 Differences between PDUs of B-ISDN and DQDB

The main distinctions between the PDUs used in B-ISDN and those used in the DQDB network are listed below:

1. The PDU formats are not identical at all hierarchical levels (see preceding sections).

2. In the DQDB network the HCS mechanism is part of the DQDB layer and covers only the QA segment header. The HEC mechanism used in B-ISDN is a function of the physical layer and it protects the entire cell header.

3. Idle slots in the DQDB network are marked by the busy bit and the slot type bit both set to zero. In B-ISDN, idle cells are identified by a predefined header pattern.

4. In B-ISDN, an explicit CLP field is included. In DQDB, a field of 2 bits is reserved for segment priority. This field is reserved for future use.

5. A predefined VCI value is used for CL services in the DQDB network.

6. Three priority levels for media access are available for a DQDB slot.

Appendix C

Abbreviations

AAL	ATM adaptation layer
AIS	Alarm indication signal
ANSI	American National Standard Institute
ATM	Asynchronous transfer mode
AU	Administrative unit
B-ISDN	Broadband integrated services digital network
B-NT1	Network termination 1 for B-ISDN
B-NT2	Network termination 2 for B-ISDN
B-TE1	Terminal equipment 1 for B-ISDN
B-TE2	Terminal equipment 2 for B-ISDN
B-TA	Terminal adaptor for B-ISDN
BER	Bit error rate
BERKOM	Berliner Kommunikationssystem
BICMOS	Bipolar complementary metal-oxide semiconductor
BIP	Bit interleaved parity
BLNT	Broadband local network technology
BOM	Beginning of message
CAD	Computer-aided design
CAM	Computer-aided manufacturing
CATV	Cable television
CBR	Constant bit rate
CCITT	Comité Consultatif International Télégraphique et Téléphonique
CIM	Computer-integrated manufacturing
CL	Connectionless
CLP	Cell loss priority
CLSF	Connectionless service functions
CMI	Coded mark inversion
CMOS	Complementary metal-oxide semiconductor
CN	Customer network
CO	Connection oriented

COM	Continuation of message
CPN	Customer premises network
CRC	Cyclic redundancy check
CS	Convergence sublayer
CSMA/CD	Carrier sense multiple access with collision detection
CSPDN	Circuit-switched public data network
DC	Direct current
DMDD	Distributed multiplexing distributed demultiplexing
DQDB	Distributed queue dual bus
DXC	Digital cross-connect
EOM	End of message
ET	Exchange termination
EWSD	Elektronisches Wählvermittlungssystem Digital
FDDI	Fibre-distributed data interface
FEBE	Far end block error
FERF	Far end receive failure
FIFO	First-in first-out
GFC	Generic flow control
HCS	Header check sequence
HDTV	High definition television
HEC	Header error control
HICOM	High technology communication
HSLAN	High speed local area network
IC	Input controller
IEEE	Institute of Electrical and Electronic Engineers
IN	Intelligent network
ISDN	Integrated services digital network
ISO	International Standard Organization
IT	Information type
IWU	Interworking unit
LAN	Local area network
LE	Local exchange
LFC	Local function capabilities
LI	Length indicator
LLS	Lan-like switching
LSB	Least significant bit
LT	Line termination
MAC	Media access control
MAN	Metropolitan area network
MID	Multiplexing identifier
MIN	Multi-path interconnection network
MSB	Most significant bit
MSVC	Meta-signalling virtual channel
MUX	Multiplexer

NNI	Network-node interface
NRZ	Non-return-to-zero code
NT	Network termination
NTSC	North American Television Standards Committee
OAM	Operation and maintenance
OAMC	Operation and maintenance centre
OC	Output controller
OSI	Open system interconnection
PACS	Picture archiving and communication system
PAL	Phase alternating line
PBX	Private branch exchange
PCI	Protocol control information
PDH	Plesiochronous digital hierarchy
PDU	Protocol data unit
PL	Physical layer
PM	Physical medium
POH	Path overhead
PON	Passive optical network
PRM	Protocol reference model
PSPDN	Packet-switched public data network
PT	Payload type
PTN	Personal telecommunications number
PTR	Pointer
RACE	Research and Development of Advanced Communication in Europe
RAM	Random access memory
RES	Reserved
QA	Queue arbitrated
QOS	Quality of service
QPSX	Queued packet and synchronous circuit exchange
SAP	Service access point
SAR	Segmentation and reassembly
SDH	Synchronous digital hierarchy
SDU	Service data unit
SECAM	Système en Couleur avec Mémoire
SIP	SMDS interface protocol
SMDS	Switched multi-megabit data service
SN	Sequence number
SNP	Sequence number protection
SOH	Section overhead
SONET	Synchronous optical network
SPN	Subscriber premises network
SSM	Single-segment message
SS7	Common channel signalling system no. 7
ST	Segment type

STM	Synchronous transfer mode
STM-i	Synchronous transport module i
SVC	Signalling virtual channel
TA	Terminal adaptor
TC	Transmission convergence sublayer
TDM	Time division multiplexing
TE	Terminal equipment
TMN	Telecommunications management network
TV	Television
UNI	User-network interface
UPT	Universal personal telecommunications
VBR	Variable bit rate
VC	Virtual channel
VC-i	Virtual container i
VCC	Virtual channel connection
VCI	Virtual channel identifier
VP	Virtual path
VPC	Virtual path connection
VPI	Virtual path identifier
WDM	Wavelength division multiplexing

Bibliography

[1] ACAMPORA, A.S., KAROL, M.J.: An Overview of Lightwave Packet Networks. *IEEE Network*, vol. 3, no. 1, January 1989, pp. 29 - 40.

[2] ADAMS, J.L.: The Orwell Torus Communication Switch. *Proceedings of the GLSB Seminar on Broadband Switching*, Albufeira, 1987, pp. 215 - 224.

[3] AHMADI, H., DENZEL, W.E.: A Survey of Modern High-Performance Switching Techniques. *IEEE Journal on Selected Areas in Communications*, vol. 7, no. 7, September 1989, pp. 1091 - 1103.

[4] ANIDO, G.J., SEETO, A.W.: Multipath Interconnection: A Technique for Reducing Congestion within Fast Packet Switching Fabrics. *IEEE Journal on Selected Areas in Communications*, vol. 6, no. 9, December 1988, pp. 1480 - 1488.

[5] ANSI: ANSI Standard 'Hybrid Ring Control'. Revision 6, May 1990.

[6] ANSI: ANSI Standard T1.105-1988 'SONET Optical Interface Rates and Formats'. 1988.

[7] ARMBRÜSTER, H., ROTHAMEL, H.-J.: Breitbandanwendungen und -dienste – Qualitative und quantitative Anforderungen an künftige Netze. *Nachrichtentechnische Zeitschrift*, vol. 43, no. 3, March 1990, pp. 150 - 159.

[8] ARMBRÜSTER, H., SCHNEIDER H.: Phasing-in the Universal Broadband ISDN: Initial Trials for Examining ATM Applications and ATM Systems. *Proceedings of the International Conference on Integrated Broadband Services and Networks*, London, 1990, pp. 200 - 205.

[9] BAIREUTHER, O.: Überlegungen zum Breitband-ISDN. *Der Fernmelde= Ingenieur*, vol. 45, no. 2/3, February/March 1991, pp. 1 - 62.

[10] BATCHER, K.E.: Sorting Networks and their Applications. *AFIPS Proceedings of the Spring Joint Computer Conference*, 1968, vol. 32, pp. 307 - 314.

[11] BELLCORE: Technical Advisory TA-TSY-000772 'Generic System Requirements in Support of Switched Multi-Megabit Data Service'. Issue 3, October 1989.

[12] More Broadband For BellSouth. *Communications Weekly International*, 1990, p. 12.

[13] BENEŠ, V.: *Mathematical Theory of Connecting Networks*. Academic Press, New York, 1965.

[14] BESIER, H.A.: SPN (Subscriber Premises Network), An Essential Part of the Broadband Communication Network. *Proceedings of the GLOBE-COM'88*, Hollywood, 1988, pp. 102 - 106.

[15] BIERSACK, E.: Principles of Network Interconnection. *Proceedings of the 7th European Fibre Optic Communications & Local Area Networks Exposition (EFOC/LAN)*, Amsterdam, 1989, pp. 37 - 43.

[16] BIOCCA, A., FRESCHI, G., FORCINA, A., MELEN, R.: Architectural Issues in the Interoperability between MANs and the ATM Network. *Proceedings of the XIII International Switching Symposium*, Stockholm, 1990, vol. II, pp. 23 - 28.

[17] BOCKER, P.: *ISDN – The Integrated Services Digital Network – Concepts, Methods, Systems*. Springer-Verlag, Berlin/Heidelberg/New York/London/Paris/Tokyo, 1988.

[18] BOULTER, R.A., POPPLE, G.W.: The Broadband User-Network Interface Projects within RACE. *Proceedings of the International Conference on Integrated Broadband Services and Networks*, London, 1990, pp. 11 - 16.

[19] BOYER, P.: A Congestion Control for the ATM. *Proceedings of the 7th International Teletraffic Congress Seminar on 'Broadband Technologies: Architectures, Applications, Control and Performance'*, Morristown, 1990.

[20] BREUER, H.-J., HELLSTRÖM, B.: Synchronous Transmission Networks. *Ericsson Review*, no. 2, 1990, pp. 60 - 71.

[21] BROOKS, E.D.: A Butterfly-Memory Interconnection for a Vector Processing Environment. *Parallel Computing*, no. 4, 1987.

[22] BYRNE, W.R., KAFKA, H.J., LUDERER, G.W.R., NELSON, B.L., CLAPP, G.H.: Evolution of Metropolitan Area Networks to Broadband ISDN. *Proceedings of the XIII International Switching Symposium*, Stockholm, 1990, vol. II, pp. 15 - 22.

[23] CCITT: COM XVIII- 228-E, Geneva, March, 1984.

[24] CCITT: COM XVIII- D1109, Hamburg, July 1987.

[25] CCITT: COM XVIII- TD6, Geneva, 1990.

[26] CCITT: COM XVIII- R41-E, Geneva, June 1990.

[27] CCITT: COM XVIII- TD11, Matsuyama, December 1990.

[28] CCITT: Recommendation G.114. 'Mean One-way Propagation Delay'. *Blue Book*, Fascicle III.1, Geneva, 1989.

[29] CCITT: Recommendation G.131. 'Stability and Echo'. *Blue Book*, Fascicle III.1, Geneva, 1989.

[30] CCITT: Recommendation G.651. 'Characteristics of a 50/125 μm Multimode Graded Index Optical Fibre Cable '. *Blue Book*, Fascicle III.3, Geneva, 1989.

[31] CCITT: Recommendation G.652. 'Characteristics of a Single Mode Optical Fibre Cable'. *Blue Book*, Fascicle III.3, Geneva, 1989.

[32] CCITT: Recommendation G.702. 'Digital Hierarchy Bit Rates'. *Blue Book*, Fascicle III.4, Geneva, 1989.

[33] CCITT: Recommendation G.703. 'Physical/Electrical Characteristics of Hierarchical Digital Interfaces'. *Blue Book*, Fascicle III.4, Geneva, 1989; Additions to G.703: see CCITT COM XVIII -R 33-E, Geneva, June 1990.

[34] CCITT: Recommendation G.707. 'Synchronous Digital Hierarchy Bit Rates'. *Blue Book*, Fascicle III.4, Geneva, 1989.

[35] CCITT: Recommendation G.708. 'Network Node Interface for the Synchronous Digital Hierarchy'. *Blue Book*, Fascicle III.4, Geneva, 1989.

[36] CCITT: Recommendation G.709. 'Synchronous Multiplexing Structure'. *Blue Book*, Fascicle III.4, Geneva, 1989.

[37] CCITT: Recommendation G.811. 'Timing Requirements at the Outputs of Primary Reference Clocks suitable for Plesiochronous Operation of International Digital Links'. *Blue Book*, Fascicle III.5, Geneva, 1989.

[38] CCITT: Recommendation G.821. 'Error Performance of an International Digital Connection forming Part of an Integrated Services Digital Network'. *Blue Book*, Fascicle III.5, Geneva, 1989.

[39] CCITT: Recommendation G.822. 'Controlled Slip Rate Objectives on an International Digital Connection'. *Blue Book*, Fascicle III.5, Geneva, 1989.

[40] CCITT: Recommendation G.823. 'The Control of Jitter and Wander within Digital Networks which are based on the 2048 kbit/s Hierarchy'. *Blue Book*, Fascicle III.5, Geneva, 1989.

[41] CCITT: Recommendation G.824. 'The Control of Jitter and Wander within Digital Networks which are based on the 1544 kbit/s Hierarchy'. *Blue Book*, Fascicle III.5, Geneva, 1989.

[42] CCITT: Recommendation G.957. 'Optical Interfaces for Equipment and Systems relating to the Synchronous Digital Hierarchy'. Geneva, July 1990.

[43] CCITT: Recommendation G.958. 'Digital Line Systems based on the Synchronous Digital Hierarchy for Use on Optical Cables'. Geneva, July 1990.

[44] CCITT: Draft Recommendation I.35B. 'Broadband ISDN Performance'. COM XVIII-TD 31 (XVIII), Matsuyama, December 1990.

[45] CCITT: Recommendation I.113. 'Vocabulary of Terms for Broadband Aspects of ISDN'. Geneva, 1991.

[46] CCITT: Recommendation I.120. 'Integrated Services Digital Networks (ISDNs)'. *Blue Book*, Fascicle III.7, Geneva, 1989.

[47] CCITT: Recommendation I.121. 'Broadband Aspects of ISDN'. Geneva, 1991.

[48] CCITT: Recommendation I.150. 'B-ISDN ATM Functional Characteristics'. Geneva, 1991.

[49] CCITT: Recommendation I.211. 'B-ISDN Service Aspects'. Geneva, 1991.

[50] CCITT: Recommendation I.311. 'B-ISDN General Network Aspects'. Geneva, 1991.

[51] CCITT: Recommendation I.320. 'ISDN Protocol Reference Model'. *Blue Book*, Fascicle III.8, Geneva, 1989.

[52] CCITT: Recommendation I.321. 'B-ISDN Protocol Reference Model and its Application'. Geneva, 1991.

[53] CCITT: Recommendation I.327. 'B-ISDN Functional Architecture'. Geneva, 1991.

[54] CCITT: Recommendation I.361. 'B-ISDN ATM Layer Specification'. Geneva, 1991.

[55] CCITT: Recommendation I.362. 'B-ISDN ATM Adaptation Layer (AAL) Functional Description'. Geneva, 1991.

[56] CCITT: Recommendation I.363. 'B-ISDN ATM Adaptation Layer (AAL) Specification'. Geneva, 1991.

[57] CCITT: Recommendation I.411. 'ISDN User-Network Interfaces – Reference Configurations'. *Blue Book*, Fascicle III.8, Geneva, 1989.

[58] CCITT: Recommendation I.412. 'ISDN User-Network Interfaces – Interface Structures and Access Capabilities'. *Blue Book*, Fascicle III.8, Geneva, 1989.

[59] CCITT: Recommendation I.413. 'B-ISDN User-Network Interface'. Geneva, 1991.

[60] CCITT: Recommendation I.430. 'Basic User-Network Interface – Layer 1 Specification'. *Blue Book*, Fascicle III.8, Geneva, 1989.

[61] CCITT: Recommendation I.431. 'Primary Rate User-Network Interface – Layer 1 Specification'. *Blue Book*, Fascicle III.8, Geneva, 1989.

[62] CCITT: Recommendation I.432. 'B-ISDN User-Network Interface – Physical Layer Specification'. Geneva, 1991.

[63] CCITT: Recommendation I.601. 'General Maintenance Principles of ISDN Subscriber Access and Subscriber Installation'. *Blue Book*, Fascicle III.9, Geneva, 1989.

[64] CCITT: Recommendation I.610. 'OAM Principles of the B-ISDN Access'. Geneva, 1991.

[65] CCITT: Recommendation M.20. 'Maintenance Philosophy for Telecommunications Networks'. *Blue Book*, Fascicle IV.1, Geneva, 1989.

[66] CCITT: Recommendation M.30. 'Principles for a Telecommunications Management Network'. *Blue Book*, Fascicle IV.1, Geneva, 1989.

[67] CCITT: Recommendation M.36. 'Principles for the Maintenance of ISDNs'. *Blue Book*, Fascicle IV.1, Geneva, 1989.

[68] CCITT: Recommendation M.60. 'Maintenance Terminology and Definitions'. *Blue Book*, Fascicle IV.1, Geneva, 1989.

[69] CCITT: Recommendation Q.761. 'Functional Description of the ISDN User Part of Signalling System No. 7'. *Blue Book*, Fascicle VI.8, Geneva, 1989.

[70] CCITT: Recommendation Q.920. 'ISDN User-Network Interface Data Link Layer - General Aspects'. *Blue Book*, Fascicle VI.10, Geneva, 1989.

[71] CCITT: Recommendation Q.921. 'ISDN User-Network Interface, Data Link Layer Specification'. *Blue Book*, Fascicle VI.10, Geneva, 1989.

[72] CCITT: Recommendation Q.922. 'A Draft Outline for an ISDN Data Link Layer Specification for Extended ISDN Applications'. Geneva, May 1990.

[73] CCITT: Recommendation Q.930. 'ISDN User-Network Interface Layer 3 - General Aspects'. *Blue Book*, Fascicle VI.11, Geneva, 1989.

[74] CCITT: Recommendation Q.931. 'ISDN User-Network Interface Layer 3 Specification for Basic Call Control'. *Blue Book*, Fascicle VI.11, Geneva, 1989.

[75] CCITT: Recommendation Q.932. 'Generic Procedures for the Control of ISDN Supplementary Services'. *Blue Book*, Fascicle VI.11, Geneva, 1989.

[76] CCITT: Recommendation Q.940. 'ISDN User-Network Interface Protocol for Management - General Aspects'. *Blue Book*, Fascicle VI.11, Geneva, 1989.

[77] CCITT: Recommendation X.1. 'International User Classes of Service in Public Data Networks and Integrated Services Digital Networks (ISDNs)'. *Blue Book*, Fascicle VIII.2, Geneva, 1989.

[78] CCITT: Recommendation X.25. 'Interface between Data Terminal Equipment (DTE) and Data Circuit-terminating Equipment (DCE) for Terminals Operating in the Packet Mode and Connected to Public Data Networks by Dedicated Circuit'. *Blue Book*, Fascicle VIII.2, Geneva, 1989.

[79] CCITT: Recommendation X.28. 'DTE/DCE Interface for a Start-Stop Mode Data Terminal Equipment accessing the Packet Assembly/Disassembly Facility (PAD) in a Public Data Network situated in the same Country'. *Blue Book*, Fascicle VIII.2, Geneva, 1989.

[80] CCITT: Recommendation X.200. 'Reference Model of Open Systems Interconnection for CCITT Applications'. *Blue Book*, Fascicle VIII.4, Geneva, 1989.

[81] CHEN, P.Y., LAWRIE, D.H., YEW, P.C., PADUA, D.A.: Interconnection Networks Using Shuffles. *IEEE Computer*, vol. 14, no. 12, December 1981, pp. 55 - 63.

[82] COUDREUSE, J.P., SERVEL, M.: PRELUDE: An Asynchronous Time-Division Switched Network. *Proceedings of the International Conference on Communications*, Seattle, 1987, paper 22.2.

[83] DAVID, R., FASTREZ, M., BAUWENS, J., DE VLEESCHOUWER, A., CHRISTIAENS, M., VAN VYVE, J.: A Belgian Broadband ATM Experiment. *Proceedings of the XIII International Switching Symposium*, Stockholm, 1990, vol. III, pp. 1 - 6.

[84] DEGAN, J.J., LUDERER, G.W.R., VAIDYA, A.K.: Fast Packet Technology for Future Switches. *AT&T Technical Journal*, vol. 68, no. 2, March/April 1989, pp. 36 - 50.

[85] DE PRYCKER, M., DE SOMER, M.: Performance of a Service Independent Switching Network with Distributed Control. *IEEE Journal on Selected Areas in Communications*, vol. 5, no. 8, October 1987, pp. 1293 - 1302.

[86] DE SMEDT, A., DE VLEESCHOUWER A., THEEUWS R.: Subscribers' Premises Networks for the Belgian Broadband Experiment. *Proceedings of the XIII International Switching Symposium*, Stockholm, 1990, vol. VI, pp. 105 - 109.

[87] DIAS D.M., KUMAR M.: Packet Switching in $n \log n$ Multistage Networks. *Proceedings of the GLOBECOM'84*, Atlanta, 1984, pp. 114 - 120.

[88] DOBROWSKI, G.H., ESTES, G.H., SPEARS, D.R., WALTERS, S.M.: Implications of BISDN Services on Network Architecture and Switching. *Proceedings of the XIII International Switching Symposium*, Stockholm, 1990, vol. I, pp. 91 - 98.

[89] ETSI: ETSI Sub Technical Committee NA5, Report of the Newcastle Meeting. November 1989.

[90] ETSI: ETSI Sub Technical Committee NA5, Report of the Rome Meeting. March 1990.

[91] FALCONER, R.M., ADAMS, J.L.: Orwell: A Protocol for an Integrated Service Local Network. *British Telecom Technology Journal*, vol. 3, no. 4, October 1985, pp. 27 - 35.

[92] FAULKNER, D.W., BALLANCE, J.W.: Passive Optical Networks for Local Telephony and Cable TV Provision. *International Journal of Digital and Analog Cabled Systems*, vol. 1, no. 3, July 1988, pp. 159 - 163.

[93] FISCHER G.: Höchste Empfängerempfindlichkeit durch optischen Über-
lagerungsempfang. *telcom report*, vol. 12, no. 4, 1989.

[94] FISCHER, W., GÖLDNER, E.-H., HUANG, N.: The Evolution from
LAN/MAN to Broadband ISDN. *Proceedings of the International Conference on Communications*, Denver, 1991, paper 39.5.

[95] FRANTZEN, V., MAHER A., ESKE CHRISTENSEN, B.: Towards the Intelligent ISDN. *Proceedings of the International Conference on Intelligent
Networks*, Bordeaux, 1989, pp. 152 - 156.

[96] GARETTI, E., MELEN, R., ARNOLD, A., GALLASSI, G., SCOZZARI, G.,
FOX, A.L., FUNDNEIDER, O., GÖLDNER, E.H.: An Experimental ATM
Switching Architecture for the Evolving B-ISDN Scenario. *Proceedings of the
XIII International Switching Symposium*, Stockholm, 1990, vol. IV, pp. 15 -
22.

[97] GECHTER, J., O'REILLY, P.: Conceptual Issues for ATM. *IEEE Network*,
vol. 3, no. 1, January 1989, pp. 14 - 16.

[98] GÖLDNER, E.H.: The Network Evolution towards B-ISDN: Applications,
Network Aspects, Trials (e.g. BERKOM). *Proceedings of the International
Conference on Communications*, Atlanta, 1990, paper 212.2.

[99] GOKE, L.R., LIPOVSKI, G.J.: Banyan Networks for Partitioning Multipro-
cessor Systems. *First Annual Symposium on Computer Architecture*, 1973,
pp. 21 - 28.

[100] HÄNDEL, R.: Evolution of ISDN towards Broadband ISDN. *IEEE Network*,
vol. 3, no. 1, January 1989, pp. 7 - 13.

[101] HÄNDEL, R., HUBER, M.N.: Customer Network Configurations and
Generic Flow Control. To appear in *International Journal of Digital and
Analog Communication Systems*.

[102] HAGENHAUS, L.: Gebührenerfassung bei ATM-Netzen. *Internal Siemens
Report*, September 1990.

[103] HAUBER, C., WALLMEIER, E.: Blocking Probabilities in ATM Pipes Controlled by a Connection Acceptance Algorithm Based on Mean and Peak Bit
Rates. *Proceedings of the XIII International Teletraffic Congress, ITC Work-
shops 'Queueing, Performance and Control in ATM'*, Copenhagen, 1991, pp.
137 - 142.

[104] HENRY, P.S.: High-Capacity Lightwave Local Area Networks. *IEEE Communications Magazine*, vol. 27, no. 10, October 1989, pp. 20 - 26.

[105] HUANG, A., KNAUER, S.: STARLITE: A Wideband Digital Switch. *Proceedings of the GLOBECOM'84*, Atlanta, 1984, pp. 121 - 125.

[106] HUBER, M.N., RATHGEB, E.P., THEIMER T.H.: Self Routing Banyan Networks in an ATM-Environment. *Proceedings of the International Conference on Computer Communication*, Tel Aviv, 1988, pp. 167 - 174.

[107] HUI, J.Y.: Resource Allocation for Broadband Networks. *IEEE Journal on Selected Areas in Communications*, vol. 6, no. 9, December 1988, pp. 1598 - 1608.

[108] IEEE: IEEE Std 802.6 - 1991: 'Distributed Queue Dual Bus (DQDB) Subnetwork of a Metropolitan Area Network (MAN)'.

[109] ISO: ISO 7498 - 1984: 'Information Processing Systems - Open System Interconnection - Basic Reference Model'. American National Standards Association, New York.

[110] ISO: ISO 8802-3 - 1990: 'Carrier Sense Multiple Access with Collision Detection (CSMA/CD) Access Method and Physical Layer Specifications'. American National Standards Association, New York.

[111] ISO: ISO 8802-4 - 1990: 'Token-passing Bus Access Method and Physical Layer Specifications'. American National Standards Association, New York.

[112] ISO: ISO 8802-5 - 1991: 'Token Ring Access Method'. American National Standards Association, New York.

[113] ISO: ISO 9314-1,-2,-3: 'Fibre Distributed Data Interface (FDDI)'. American National Standards Association, New York.

[114] KAROL, M.J., HLUCHYI, M.G., MORGAN, S.P.: Input versus Output Queueing on a Space-division Packet Switch. *IEEE Transactions on Communications*, vol. 35, no. 12, December 1987, pp. 1347 - 1356.

[115] KAMMERL, A.: Contribution on Echo Control. Submitted to CEPT/NA5 Meeting in Madeira, October 1988.

[116] KIMURA, T., SAITO, S.: Coherent Lightwave Communications – Overview. *Proceedings of the International Conference on Communications*, Philadelphia, 1988, paper 37.1.1.

[117] KRÖNER, H.: Comparative Performance Study of Space Priority Mechanisms for ATM Networks. *Proceedings of the INFOCOM'90*, San Francisco, 1990, pp. 1136 - 1143.

[118] KUEHN, P.J.: From ISDN to IBCN (Integrated Broadband Communication Network). *Proceedings of the World Computer Congress IFIP'89*, San Francisco, 1989, pp. 479 - 486.

[119] LAMPE, D.: Transfer Delay Deviation of Packets in ATD Switching Matrices and its Effect on Dimensioning a Depacketizer Buffer. *Proceedings of the International Conference on Computer Communication*, Tel Aviv, 1988, pp. 55 - 60.

[120] LEA, C.T.: Multi-log$_2$ N Self-Routing Networks and their Applications in High Speed Electronic and Photonic Switching Systems. *Proceedings of the INFOCOM'89*, Ottawa, 1989, pp. 877 - 886.

[121] LUDERER, G.W.R., KNAUER, S.C.: The Evolution of Space Division Packet Switches. *Proceedings of the XIII International Switching Symposium*, Stockholm, 1990, vol. V, pp. 211 - 216.

[122] LUTZ, K.A.: Considerations on ATM Switching Techniques. *International Journal of Digital and Analog Cabled Systems*, vol. 1, no. 4, October 1988, pp. 237 - 243.

[123] MÖHRMANN, K.H.: Kupfer oder Glasfaser zum Teilnehmer – Wettbewerb oder Ergänzung? *Tagungsband zur VDI/VDE-Tagung Verbindungstechnik'91*, Karlsruhe 1991.

[124] MOLLENAUER, J.F: Standards of Metropolitan Area Networks. *IEEE Communications Magazine*, vol. 26, no. 4, April 1988, pp. 15 - 19.

[125] MÜLLER, H.R., NASSEHI, M.M., WONG, J.W., ZURFLUH, E., BUX, W., ZAFIROPULO, P.: DQMA and CRMA: New Access Schemes for Gbit/s LANs and MANs. *Proceedings of the INFOCOM'90*, San Francisco, 1990, pp. 185 - 191.

[126] NEWMAN, R.M., BUDRIKIS, Z.L., HULLETT J.L.: The QPSX Man. *IEEE Communications Magazine*, vol. 26, no. 4, April 1988, pp. 20 - 28.

[127] NUSSBAUM, E.: Communication Network Needs and Technologies – A Place for Photonic Switching? *IEEE Journal on Selected Areas in Communications*, vol. 6, no. 7, August 1988, pp. 1036 - 1043.

[128] OIE, Y., MURATA, M., KUBOTA, K., MIYAHARA, H.: Effect of Speedup in Nonblocking Packet Switches. *Proceedings of the International Conference on Communications*, Boston, 1989, pp. 410 - 414.

[129] PATEL, J.H.: Performance of Processor-Memory Interconnection for Multiprocessors. *IEEE Transactions on Computers*, vol. 30, no. 10, October 1981, pp. 771 - 780.

[130] POPESCU-ZELETIN, R., EGLOFF, P., BUTSCHER, B.: BERKOM – A Broadband ISDN Project. *Proceedings of the International Zurich Seminar*, Zürich, 1988, paper B5.

[131] RACE: RACE Project R1044/2.10 Broadband User/Network Interface BUNI, 4th Deliverable 'Interface Specification – Draft A and Rationale'. *British Telecom Research Laboratories*, Martlesham Heath, November 1989.

[132] RATHGEB, E.P., THEIMER, T.H., HUBER, M.N.: Buffering Concepts for ATM Switching Networks. *Proceedings of the GLOBECOM'88*, Hollywood, 1988, pp. 1277 - 1281.

[133] RATHGEB, E.P., THEIMER, T.H., HUBER, M.N.: ATM Switches – Basic Architectures and their Performance. *International Journal of Digital and Analog Cabled Systems*, vol. 2, no. 4, October 1989, pp. 227 - 236.

[134] RATHGEB, E.P.: Policing Mechanisms for ATM Networks – Modelling and Performance Comparison. *Proceedings of the 7th International Teletraffic Congress Seminar on 'Broadband Technologies: Architectures, Applications, Control and Performance'*, Morristown, 1990, paper 10.1.

[135] ROTHERMEL, K., SEEGER, D.: Traffic Studies of Switching Networks for Asynchronous Tranfer Mode (ATM). *Proceedings of the 12th International Teletraffic Congress*, Torino, 1988, paper 1.3A.5.

[136] SCHAFFER, B.: ATM Switching in the Developing Telecommunication Network. *Proceedings of the XIII International Switching Symposium*, Stockholm, 1990, vol. I, pp. 105 - 110.

[137] SCHOUTE, F.C.: Simple Decision Rules for Acceptance of Mixed Traffic Streams. *Proceedings of the 12th International Teletraffic Congress*, Torino, 1988, paper 4.2A.5.

[138] SIEMENS: The Intelligent Integrated Broadband Network – Telecommunications in the 1990s. Siemens, München, 1989.

[139] SUNSHINE, C.A.: Network Interconnection and Gateways. *IEEE Journal on Selected Areas in Communications*, vol. 8, no. 1, December 1990, pp. 4 - 11.

[140] THEIMER, T.H.: Performance Comparison of Routing Strategies in ATM Switches. *Proceedings of the XIII International Teletraffic Congress*, Copenhagen, 1991, pp. 923 - 928.

[141] TOBAGI, F.A.: Fast Packet Switch Architectures For Broadband Integrated Services Digital Networks. *Proceedings of the IEEE*, vol. 78, no. 1, January 1990, pp. 133 - 167.

[142] TURNER, J.S.: Design of a Broadcast Packet Switching Network. *IEEE Transactions on Communications*, vol. 36, no. 6, June 1987, pp. 734 - 743.

[143] VODHANEL, R.S., WAGNER, R.E.: Multi-gigabit/sec Coherent Lightwave Systems. *Proceedings of the International Conference on Communications*, Boston, 1989, paper 14.4.1.

[144] VORSTERMANS, J.P., DE VLEESCHOUWER, A.P.: Layered ATM Systems and Architectural Concepts for Subscribers' Premises Networks. *IEEE Journal on Selected Areas in Communications*, vol. 6, no. 9, December 1988, pp. 1545 - 1555.

[145] WIEST, G.: More Intelligence and Flexibility for Communication Network – Challenges for Tomorrow's Switching Systems. *Proceedings of the XIII International Switching Symposium*, Stockholm, 1990, vol. V, pp. 201 - 204.

[146] WU, C.L., FENG, T.Y.: On a Class of Multistage Interconnection Networks. *IEEE Transactions on Computers*, vol. 29, no. 8, August 1980, pp. 694 - 702.

[147] ZITSEN, W.: Metropolitan Area Networks: Taking LANs into the Public Network. *Telecommunications*, June 1990, pp. 53 - 60.

Index

AAL (ATM adaptation layer) 53, 57, 92
AAL protocol 58
AAL type 1 92
AAL type 2 94
AAL type 3 96
AAL type 4 100
access configuration 107
access network 146
accounting management 186
activation/deactivation 83, 157
add/drop capability 61
addressing 163
adjacent layer protocol 50
alarm indication signal 107
application layer 52
assured operation 97, 100
asynchronous transfer mode (ATM) 5, 14, 16
ATM adaptation layer (AAL) 53, 57, 92
ATM connection 19, 35, 89, 103
ATM cross-connect 57, 107, 140, 147
ATM island 175
ATM layer 15, 20, 39, 44, 53, 54, 57, 59, 83, 103
ATM multiplexer 37, 139
ATM network performance 32
ATM performance parameter 31
ATM primitive 59
ATM speech 175
ATM switch 30, 37, 57, 113, 157, 169
ATM transport network 20, 23, 26, 39
ATM-izing 137, 156, 157
attenuation 80, 81
authentication 191
average bit rate 33, 36, 37

bandwidth allocation 16, 37
Banyan network 127, 131
  (L)-level 127
  irregular 127
  regular 127
  SW- 128
baseline network 128, 132
basic access 2, 62
basic access signal 157
beginning of message 95, 98, 99, 174
Beneš network 133
bidelta network 128
bit alignment 56
bit error 75, 76, 92
bit error probability 18, 76, 78, 147
bit error multiplication 80
bit interleaved parity 110
bit rate
  average 33, 36, 37
  peak 33, 36, 37, 178
bit sequence independence 80, 141
bit timing 56, 78, 141
bit-by-bit check 77
B-NT1 63
B-NT2 63
  centralized 44
  distributed 44
B-NT2 function 64
bridge 163
broadband application 7
broadband definition 4
broadband service 7, 13, 26, 155
broadband terminal 65, 87
buffer
  first-in first-out 115
  random access 115
buffer dimensioning 37
buffering mechanism 35
burstiness 33, 37
bus 44, 46, 64, 66, 68, 144, 146, 159
  dual 68
  passive 62, 66

Notes

Notes